More Advance Praise for
Guantánamo: What the World Should Know

"Guantánamo Bay used to be a symbol of liberty or of capitalist recalcitrance, depending on your view of Fidel Castro. Today it is the foremost symbol of American arrogance. The name alone is now sufficient to elicit disbelief, even from our staunchest allies. Michael Ratner is the perfect guide to this strange new world. In a lively, highly accessible conversation with Ellen Ray, he makes the complex simple and the convoluted clear. We come away from our exposure to this noted activist feeling both enlightened and outraged. And we feel one thing more: that it is good to live in a world with a Michael Ratner in it."
—**William F. Schulz, executive director,**
Amnesty International USA

"The chasm between constitutional ideal and actual policy that Guantánamo opens up is one more illustration of the capacity for absolute power to corrupt absolutely. Ratner and Ray at least give us the facts we need to solidify our own stand against the Bush administration's neo-medievalism. Feel outraged, then get active."
—**Dame Anita Roddick, author, activist,**
and founder of The Body Shop

"From Anthony Lewis's compelling introduction, 'A President Beyond the Law,' through the appendices documenting U.S.-Cuban agreements, *Guantánamo,* with its panorama of prisoner abuse, should be required reading for any American who considers himself a patriot and a defender of human rights."
—**Rose Styron, poet, journalist, and human rights activist**

"A brilliant and eloquent indictment of our current administration's disrespect for basic human rights. Ratner breaks down what Guantánamo is, why it matters, and the ramifications for national and international law. This book should be required reading for those concerned with truth, justice, and maintaining our humanity."
—**Rachel Neumann, rights and liberties editor, AlterNet.org**

GUANTÁNAMO

GUANTÁNAMO

What the World Should Know

Michael Ratner and Ellen Ray

With "A President Beyond the Law" by Anthony Lewis

A POLITICS OF THE LIVING BOOK

CHELSEA GREEN PUBLISHING
WHITE RIVER JUNCTION, VERMONT

Designed by Peter Holm, Sterling Hill Productions

Printed in Canada
First printing, June 2004

10 9 8 7 6 5 4 3 2 1

Printed on acid-free, recycled paper

Library of Congress Cataloging-in-Publication Data

Ratner, Michael, 1943-
Guantánamo : What the World Should Know / Michael Ratner and Ellen Ray.
p. cm. – (A politics of the living book)
ISBN 1-931498-64-4 (pbk.)
1. Prisoners of war–Legal status, laws, etc. 2. Combatants and
noncombatants (International law) 3. War on Terrorism, 2001—Law and
legislation–United States. 4. Military bases, American–Law and
legislation–Cuba. 5. Guantánamo Bay Naval Base (Cuba) 6. Geneva
Conventions (1949) I. Ray, Ellen. II. Title. III. Politics of the living.
KZ6495.R38 2004
973.931–dc22

2004012395

Chelsea Green Publishing Company
Post Office Box 428
White River Junction, VT 05001
(800) 639-4099
www.chelseagreen.com

Contents

"A PRESIDENT BEYOND THE LAW"

The question tears at all of us, regardless of party or ideology: How could American men and women treat Iraqi prisoners with such cruelty—and laugh at their humiliation? We are told that there was a failure of military leadership. Officers in the field were lax. Pentagon officials didn't care. So the worst in human nature was allowed to flourish.

But something much more profound underlies this terrible episode. It is a culture of low regard for the law, of respecting the law only when it is convenient.

Again and again, over these last years, President Bush has made clear his view that law must bend to what he regards as necessity. National security as he defines it trumps our commitments to international law. The Constitution must yield to novel infringements on American freedom.

One clear example is the treatment of the prisoners at Guantánamo Bay, Cuba. The Third Geneva Convention requires that any dispute about a prisoner's status be decided by a "competent tribunal." American forces provided many such tribunals for prisoners taken in the Persian Gulf War in 1991. But Mr. Bush has refused to comply with the Geneva Convention. He decided that all the Guantánamo prisoners were "unlawful combatants"—that is, not regular soldiers but spies, terrorists or the like.

The Supreme Court is now considering whether the prisoners can use American courts to challenge their designation as unlawful. The administration's brief could not be blunter in its argument that the president is the law on this issue: "The president, in his capacity as commander in chief, has conclusively determined that the Guantánamo detainees . . . are not entitled to prisoner-of-war status under the Geneva Convention."

The violation of the Geneva Convention and that refusal to let the courts consider the issue have cost the United States dearly in the world legal community—the judges and lawyers in societies that, historically, have looked to the United States as the exemplar of a country committed to law. Lord Steyn, a judge on Britain's highest court, condemned the administration's position on Guantánamo in an address last fall—pointing out that American courts would refuse even to hear claims of torture from prisoners. At the time, the idea of torture at Guantánamo seemed far-fetched to me. After the disclosures of the last 10 days, can we be sure?

Instead of a country committed to law, the United States is now seen as a country that proclaims high legal ideals and then says that they should apply to all others but not to itself. That view has been worsened by the Bush administration's determination that Americans not be subject to the new International Criminal Court, which is supposed to punish genocide and war crimes.

Fear of terrorism—a quite understandable fear after 9/11—has led to harsh departures from normal legal practice at home. Aliens swept off the streets by the Justice Department as possible terrorists after 9/11 were subjected to physical abuse and humiliation by prison guards, the department's inspector general found. Attorney General John Ashcroft did not apologize—a posture that sent a message.

Inside the United States, the most radical departure from law as we have known it is President Bush's claim that he can designate any American citizen an "enemy combatant"—and thereupon detain that person in solitary confinement indefinitely, without charges, without a trial, without a right to counsel. Again, the president's lawyers have argued determinedly that he must have the last word, with little or no scrutiny from lawyers and judges.

There was a stunning moment in President Bush's 2003 State of the Union address when he said that more than 3,000 suspected terrorists "have been arrested in many countries. And many others have met a different fate. Let's put it this way: They are no longer a problem for the United States."

In all these matters, there is a pervasive attitude: that to follow the law is to be weak in the face of terrorism. But commitment to law is not a weakness. It has been the great strength of the United States from the beginning. Our leaders depart from that commitment at their peril, and ours, for a reason that Justice Louis D. Brandeis memorably expressed 75 years ago.

"Our government is the potent, the omnipresent teacher," he wrote. "For good or ill, it teaches the whole people by its example. Crime is contagious. If the government becomes a lawbreaker, it breeds contempt for the law; it invites every man to become a law unto himself."

—Anthony Lewis
May 7, 2004

INTERVIEWER'S PREFACE

It was late summer 2003 when I agreed to ask my friend Michael Ratner to participate in a book project for Margo Baldwin of Chelsea Green Publishing about the legal plight of the prisoners held in the ultra-secret facilities at the Guantánamo Bay Naval Station in Cuba. Michael, a human rights attorney and the president of the Center for Constitutional Rights (CCR), was, as he explains below, a Gitmo veteran of sorts. Our passionate publisher Margo convinced us to use an interview technique to explain a very complicated, developing situation, as had been used in the book by William Rivers Pitt and Scott Ritter, *War on Iraq,* which she helped publish.

Few people outside the Pentagon knew anything about what was happening at Guantánamo. Shortly after 9/11, thousands of Muslims and Arabs, all allegedly very dangerous terrorists, had been rounded up, and hundreds, from more than forty countries, were transported to Guantánamo. The conditions they were being held in were unknown; the base was totally off-limits to journalists, researchers, and human-rights activists. The Pentagon had classified who was there, why, how many of them there were, where they came from, and most importantly, what was being done to them.

As one of the few civilians knowledgeable about Guantánamo, Michael Ratner, along with his colleagues at the Center for

Constitutional Rights and elsewhere, began representing several of the prisoners whose families had managed to learn of their plight and seek legal assistance. But aside from a few prisoner letters and an unusual International Committee of the Red Cross (ICRC) report describing the mental state of the prisoners there as universally "in despair," we had little direct information about the treatment the prisoners had received. At first our manuscript was replete with terms like "alleged brutality," "claims of torture," "possible deaths by beating."

Events then overtook us. Between March and May of 2004, as we were conducting the interviews that comprise the text of this book, the world was confronted with the photos of the sadistic torture and mistreatment of Iraqi prisoners at Abu Ghraib. Allegations became facts. Initial denials of any systematic misconduct, or of approval or direction by military officers or Bush administration officials, began to dissolve in a swirl of contrary evidence, which continues today.

In the fall of 2003, Major General Geoffrey D. Miller, at that time the commander of Guantánamo Bay Naval Station, was sent to Iraq by the Pentagon's intelligence chief to "Gitmoize" Abu Ghraib prison there. This meant "facilitating" interrogations by having low-level military police guards "soften up" the prisoners, "enabling" the intelligence interrogators to get confessions, apparently by any means necessary, ignoring the Geneva Conventions.

The connection between Abu Ghraib and what many suspected had gone on at Guantánamo became clearer as the military was forced to release some of those detained at Guantánamo, whose subsequent accounts echoed the Abu Ghraib abuses. Further reports by the ICRC, the Pentagon, and the State Department, White House memos, and endless interviews and congressional hearings document the horrendous abuses about which the entire story has yet to be written.

The other manner in which events overtook us was that the

Supreme Court granted review of the lower court cases relating to
the legal rights of the prisoners at Guantánamo and the two U.S.
citizens being held in military prisons as "enemy combatants."
This book has gone to press after the arguments but before the
Court's decisions. As the reader will note, we have had to specu-
late on those results.

Regardless of the legal impact of the Supreme Court's rulings,
it is clear that the remaining prisoners will need whatever protection can be provided by having the eyes of the world upon their
captors. We hope this book will play a small part in helping its
readers to understand the horrors that are being committed by the
U.S. administration and to take action against them.

—Ellen Ray

INTERVIEWEE'S PREFACE

I have had a lot of experience with Guantánamo. In the early 1990s, I was one of the counsel from the Center for Constitutional Rights representing Haitian refugees imprisoned in an HIV camp at Guantánamo Bay Naval Station in Cuba. I visited my clients and the base a number of times. It was a dreadful experience, a desert outpost where inhuman treatment, even of refugees, was common practice. It was in the litigation regarding those refugees that the U.S. government, initially under the presidency of George H. W. Bush, formulated its legal position that Guantánamo was a law-free zone. According to the first Bush administration, the Constitution simply did not apply at Guantánamo.

Although our team of lawyers ultimately prevailed in the case, the administration was insistent that Guantánamo remain a law-free zone, preserving a territory in the world where the U.S. government was free from court scrutiny, free from the constraints of the Constitution, and free, sadly, to violate people's rights with impunity.

Yet in January 2002, when I read that the first prisoners from the Afghanistan war and from President Bush's "war on terror" were being sent to Guantánamo, I was still shocked. I knew what it meant. It meant not only a tough legal fight to protect their rights, but also that there would be no check on the treatment of those detained. They would be imprisoned without any right to see, speak to, or write to lawyers; without visits from family members; and without any charges specified against them. The administration was painting all of them—falsely, it turns out—as the "worst of the worst," ordering their imprisonment until the war on terror was over, a period that might easily run some fifty years.

Whether the Center for Constitutional Rights should get involved was not the easiest of decisions. But we saw these detentions as an extremely serious assault on our fundamental liberties. We believed strongly that the president, acting unilaterally, did not have the right, even as commander in chief in a war, simply to designate people for detention, hold them incommunicado, deny court review, and throw away the key. At that time we could not even imagine the abuses that have now been revealed.

We began to round up other lawyers to work with us, but it was not an easy task. The only lawyers willing to help were anti-death-penalty lawyers who were used to representing unpopular clients. And we got plenty of hate mail, especially early on, for our representation of the Guantánamo detainees.

As is explained in this book, we lost our case at the trial level, in U.S. district court, and we lost our appeal to the circuit court. But to our great surprise, the Supreme Court granted review, and arguments were heard on April 20, 2004. It went well, but there will not be a decision until after this book goes to press. I am optimistic that the courthouse door will not be closed to those imprisoned by the United States at Guantánamo and that the Court will reaffirm the principle that we are a country of laws where people cannot be imprisoned at the whim of the chief executive.

Only days after the Supreme Court argument, the notorious Abu Ghraib pictures were publicly revealed. And it is becoming clear that such abuses, mistreatment, and torture are rampant in other U.S. military prisons—perhaps many others. Our work to expose and stop this is only beginning. Whatever euphemisms they may use—such as "stress and duress"—officials in the U.S. government have committed war crimes. We hope this book will stand as a warning of the risks the United States takes when it departs from the rule of law, from rules of civilized conduct.

I want to thank Ellen Ray, my good friend, who took my files, read and analyzed them, and forced me to sit down to be interviewed. Her husband, William Schaap, a lawyer and editor, also did masterful work on the manuscript. And our publisher, Margo Baldwin, pushed us to make sure our message was as timely as possible.

Joe Marguiles from Minneapolis, a cooperating attorney with CCR, became a key litigator in what ultimately became a Supreme Court case. Two other lawyers who were most helpful early on were Clive Stafford Smith from Louisiana and Professor Eric M. Freedman from Hofstra University. Each of them played a remarkable role as the litigation went forward. I also want to thank Shearman & Sterling and its lead counsel, Thomas Wilmer, a terrific and determined lawyer. And I must thank the British lawyers, especially Gareth Pierce and Louise Christian, and the courageous military defense attorneys with whom we worked.

Finally, I want to express my gratitude to the Center for Constitutional Rights and its lawyers and staff for working so hard on the Guantánamo cases. Attorneys Barbara Olshanky, Steven Watt, and Jules Lobel all played important roles in the litigation. CCR has been instrumental in fighting for people's rights since its beginnings, when it defended civil rights activists in the south in the time of Martin Luther King, Jr. It has been one of the leading legal institutions fighting for our rights since 9/11. Not only is the Center lead counsel in the Guantánamo cases, but it is representing, in a class action, Muslim and Arab detainees arrested in the Ashcroft sweeps in the United States that followed 9/11, and it is legal counsel to Maher Arar, the Canadian citizen "rendered" to Syria, where he was tortured. CCR also won the first case declaring a section of the Patriot Act unconstitutional. As I write this, in June 2004, CCR has just launched a major case against private contractors allegedly involved in torturing detainees in Iraq and Guantánamo.

—Michael Ratner

CHAPTER ONE

GUANTÁNAMO AND RULE BY EXECUTIVE FIAT

Guantánamo Explained

Ellen Ray: Michael, the American military base at Guantánamo Bay, Cuba, has been called everything from "an off-shore concentration camp" to a "legal black hole." What is happening there and why is it so important we have this discussion about it?

Michael Ratner: Guantánamo has become a symbol of much that is wrong with our society. It is a complex of brutal prisons where hundreds of men and boys from all over the world, many of whom we believe are neither guilty of any crime nor pose any danger to the security of the United States, are being held by the U.S. government under incredibly inhuman conditions and incessant interrogation. They have not been charged with anything, they have no access to counsel or the courts, no right to any hearing of any kind, and no idea when, if ever, they will see an end to their plight. These prisons are a symbol of the disdain with which the Bush administration has brushed aside long-standing precepts of international law and civilized conduct. It is indeed a national disgrace.

Ray: To begin this examination of Guantánamo, tell us something about the history of this base.

Ratner: Guantánamo Bay Naval Station, a U.S. military base comprising 45 square miles at Guantánamo Bay, Cuba, exists as a result of what one might call the first phase of outward U.S. imperialism (as opposed to inward imperialism, the so-called manifest destiny under which the United States conquered much of North America). For a very long time, the United States had coveted some Spanish colonies—in particular Cuba and Puerto Rico, neither very far from Florida. In 1898, as Cuba was fighting for its independence against Spain, the United States intervened in what became the Spanish-American War under the guise of helping the Cubans defeat the Spanish. A little less than a year later, when the war ended, the United States controlled Cuba, Puerto Rico, the Philippines, and several other former Spanish colonies.

Cuba's constitution, which was adopted in 1901, included what is called the Platt Amendment (see Appendix One: Documents), legislation that established conditions for American intervention in Cuba and gave the United States the right to maintain a military base on the island in perpetuity.

Pursuant to the Platt Amendment, in 1903 the United States leased Guantánamo from Cuba (see Appendix One: Documents). The lease contains several critical provisions relevant to whether U.S. courts have jurisdiction over the base. First, the lease gives the United States "complete jurisdiction and control" of that territory, saying merely that it "recognizes the continuance of the ultimate sovereignty of the Republic of Cuba." In other words, the Cubans have no authority whatsoever over Guantánamo.

Secondly, the lease can only be terminated on the mutual consent of both parties. Even though Cuba has wanted to terminate the lease since the revolution in 1959, it is unable to do so without the consent of the United States. And the United States can withhold its consent forever.

The lease actually provides for a minuscule rent, some two

thousand dollars in gold (equivalent to about $4,085 a year in current U.S. dollars), although the Cuban government has refused to accept any payment since 1959. The United States is technically in default, and has been for many years, because the lease provides that the base is to be used only for a coaling station; but the Cubans have never been able to do anything about this. The base has been used as everything from a holding pen for Haitian refugees to a prison for the Guantánamo detainees—everything except its original purpose as a coaling station.

The United States claims it does not have sovereignty over the Guantánamo base, but in fact it exercises all aspects of sovereignty. For all intents and purposes, Guantánamo is a colony or territory of the United States. A U.S. soldier who commits a crime in Guantánamo—rape, murder, or something else—can be tried by a court-martial in Guantánamo or can be brought into the United States and tried in a federal district court. The applicable law in Guantánamo is the federal U.S. law. The United States has complete control and jurisdiction over Guantánamo, which should give American courts the authority to look into the detentions in Guantánamo.

Ray: In its current incarnation, what is Guantánamo Bay Naval Station, in fact?

Ratner: Guantánamo is something vastly different from what the average American would think of as a prison. Guantánamo is a twenty-first century Pentagon experiment that was, in fact, outlawed by the Geneva Conventions of 1949. It is similar in purpose to the German World War II operations that led to the ban: it is an interrogation camp, and interrogation camps are completely and flatly illegal.

Guantánamo has provided an opportunity for the U.S. government to hold people outside any legal or moral system, with no access to lawyers or contact with family, in dehumanizing isolation, and subject to physical duress, psychological manipulation, and in some cases conduct that may amount to torture. The detainees have no means of asserting their innocence and no means of testing their detentions in any court. In the case that the Center for Constitutional Rights brought, the lower federal courts ruled that the detainees had no right to file a writ of habeas corpus.

Ray: Before we go further, perhaps you should explain just what a writ of habeas corpus is.

Ratner: This is essentially a request to a court to order an official under whose authority a person is being detained to bring that prisoner before the court in order to justify the lawfulness of that detention to the court. It has been a hallmark of Anglo-American law dating back to the seventeenth century, when some British officials were sending prisoners to remote islands and military bases to prevent any judicial inquiry into their imprisonment. Parliament passed the Habeas Corpus Act to prohibit this practice of offshore penal colonies beyond the reach of the law—precisely the practice the Bush administration has revived.

Ray: What purpose does Guantánamo serve?

Ratner: Guantánamo's purpose is to break down the human personalities of the detainees in order to coerce from them whatever their captors want, to get them to confess to anything, to implicate anyone. Guantánamo is a prison where cruel and inhuman and degrading treatment—even torture—is practiced, and it is utterly illegal.

That is what Guantánamo is and has been for almost three years. The U.S. government admits it is an interrogation camp, though it denies torture is used there. However, the administration admits to using techniques that legally constitute cruel, inhuman, and degrading treatment, which is prohibited under law. Interrogation is why the U.S. administration is depriving all these people of any legal or human rights, why it shaves their heads and keeps them in cages, why they have no access to their families, why in many cases their families may not even know if they are dead or alive.

Ray: Why should American citizens be concerned about Guantánamo and what is taking place there?

Ratner: Americans should care about what goes on at Guantánamo for a number of reasons. First of all, the way we are treating the prisoners there is a scandal, an embarrassment to the people of this country and an outrage to the people of the world. That you can take someone and put him in a prison off-shore with no legal rights whatsoever for two and a half years is simply inhumane.

Second, our treatment of these people, who are primarily Muslims and of Arabic ethnic origin, should be a cause of tremendous consternation because of the message it sends to the Muslim world. Guantánamo has become iconic in the Arab and Muslim world; it stands for the United States doing wrong and abusing people.

If we want to live in a safe world, the message we should send is that we will treat people not like animals but like human beings. Although we should be trying to lessen the anger toward the United States within the Muslim and Arab world, we are not doing that; we are, in fact, doing the opposite.

Third, we should care about Guantánamo because we should care about how others are going to treat our citizens. If Americans—soldiers or civilians—are picked up overseas, how do we want them to be treated? Do we want them treated lawfully, in accordance with either criminal law or the Geneva

Conventions, or do we want them treated like we are treating the prisoners at Guantánamo? The United States is setting an example for how international prisoners are to be treated, and it is a terrible example.

A fourth reason we should care is what this all means for the future of the rule of law, and for the building of societies that are based upon the rule of law and not on the dictates of kings or presidents. For nearly eight hundred years, since the signing of the Magna Carta in 1215, our laws have insisted that every single human being is entitled to some kind of judicial process before he or she can be thrown in jail. The United States is trying to overturn one of the most fundamental principles of Anglo-American jurisprudence and international law. This is a principle that is found in the Declaration of the Rights of Man, in the Universal Declaration of Human Rights, and in the International Covenant on Civil and Political Rights.

We have gone back to a pre-Magna Carta medieval system, not a system of laws, but of executive fiat, where the king—or in this case the president—simply decides, on any particular day, I'm going to throw you into some prison. You are not going to have access to a lawyer or anybody else, or even know if there are any charges against you, or if you will ever be released from this prison. Guantánamo has become our Devil's Island, our Château d'If from *The Count of Monte Cristo*.

The consequences of this unilateral abrogation of fundamental law are grave, not merely for the people in Guantánamo and for citizens of other countries, but also for every person in the United States. If we care about civilization and the rule of law and justice, we cannot keep treating people like this. There should be no place in the world that is a law-free zone, no place in the world where human beings have no rights.

The Center for Constitutional Rights's Involvement

Ray: How did the Center for Constitutional Rights become involved in the defense of the Guantánamo prisoners?

Ratner: It happens that I live very close to the site of the World Trade Center, and like many others I was utterly shocked and distraught after the September 11 attacks.

But early on, my colleagues at the Center and I saw that this act was going to be used by the Bush administration as an excuse for draconian restrictions of our civil rights and civil liberties at home and for expanded U.S. hegemony and warmaking abroad. September 11 has become an excuse—whether in Guantánamo, in Afghanistan, in Iraq, or here at home—for the wholesale infringement of fundamental liberties. For example, by November 2001, the police and the FBI had already arrested and detained, by some estimates, up to three thousand Muslim or Arab noncitizens in the United States. These people were not even suspected of terrorism; they were merely non-U.S. citizens who had allegedly violated some immigration procedure. Many of these people effectively disappeared in U.S. jails; a number were beaten and ultimately deported. It was a real sign of times to come. The Center began a major case, *Turkmen v. Ashcroft,* that challenged these detentions.

We then started to put together a team of lawyers to represent some of those who might be imprisoned at Guantánamo naval base in Cuba. The first case came quickly. We spoke to a lawyer in Australia, Stephen Kenny, who was representing an Australian citizen who had been imprisoned, David Hicks. He asked us to represent Hicks in the federal habeas corpus suits we were planning, and this became our first case.

The atmosphere in the United States in January 2002 was so fearful and intimidating that we could not get a single other legal organization to join with the Center. We had great difficulty getting local counsel in Washington to help us argue that Hicks's detention was illegal. And when it became known that I was representing him, I got the worst hate mail I have ever received. I got letters asking me why I didn't just let the Taliban come to my house and eat my children.

Nevertheless, we finally filed for a writ of habeas corpus in the federal district court in the District of Columbia, on behalf of Hicks and two young men from England, Shafiq Rasul and Asif Iqbal. Subsequently we added Mamdouh Habib, another Australian who had been picked up in Pakistan and shipped to Guantánamo via Egypt, where we believe he was tortured. In the meantime, similar claims were being raised by a private law firm hired by the Kuwaiti government on behalf of a dozen Kuwaiti citizens detained at Guantánamo.

The administration's principal argument was that no alien held by the United States outside the United States has the right to litigate his detention in a U.S. court. That is, if you are an alien being held at a U.S. base in Guantánamo, Cuba, or Bagram, Afghanistan, or the island of Diego Garcia in the Indian Ocean, you can't come into an American court, period. Such aliens have no right to habeas corpus and no constitutional rights at all. No First Amendment right to speak; no Fourth Amendment right to be protected against unlawful detention; no Fifth Amendment right against self-incrimination; no right to due process; no right to any kind of a hearing to test their detention.

We thought this argument was very wrong. We believe that any person detained or jailed by the United States has a right to test the legality of his or her detention in a U.S. court. And, even if somehow that broad proposition was not the case, a person detained at Guantánamo certainly has that right. The United States exercises all power in Guantánamo, and the writ of habeas corpus should certainly apply there. Only U.S. courts can protect people's rights in Guantánamo. No other country's courts in the world can do so.

Ray: How did the war in Afghanistan lead to the detentions in Guantánamo?

Ratner: What happened when the U.S. military went into Afghanistan in October 2001 was extraordinary. As Secretary of Defense Donald Rumsfeld put it, they "scooped up ten thousand people." Those were not necessarily people found on the battlefield. Many were from Pakistan and the surrounding areas; many were in civilian clothes; many were taken in midnight raids that had nothing to do with the Taliban or with al Qaeda. And most of them were picked up not by U.S. forces but by the Northern Alliance, a loose coalition in a small corner of Afghanistan whom the Taliban had been fighting to oust.

The Northern Alliance, in conjunction with a bunch of warlords, eventually picked up as many as 35,000 or 40,000 people. The United States was dropping leaflets all over the country offering rewards of anywhere from $50 to $5,000 for members of al Qaeda and high-level Taliban officials. In Afghanistan, these were huge sums of money. Villagers and warlords, including members of the Northern Alliance, started turning over their enemies or anyone they didn't like, or finally, anyone they could pick up. Among those who have been released are taxi drivers and even a shepherd in his nineties.

We don't know everything about what happened to the thousands of people who were eventually turned over to or captured by the United States. Initially, many were sent to detention facilities in Bagram and Kandahar, Afghanistan, where the first interrogations took place. A number of detainees reported being beaten at these facilities, and there are reliable reports that techniques amounting to torture were employed. John Walker Lindh, the so-called American Taliban, was strapped naked to a gurney and spent two days in a shipping container.

Some detainees were apparently sent to third countries in a process called "rendition." U.S. authorities knew that torture would be used by the security services of those countries to obtain information. One of CCR's clients, for instance, was sent first to Egypt where he was apparently tortured and then sent on to Guantánamo.

Beginning in January 2002, hundreds of these prisoners were transported to Guantánamo. The prisoners included some people picked up outside of the so-called war zone of Afghanistan and Pakistan, in places like Bosnia, Zambia, and Gambia.

Ray: Once they picked up all of these people in Afghanistan and Pakistan, what should they have done with them?

Ratner: Whether you agreed with the administration's policy or not, a state of war existed between the U.S. government and the Taliban government of Afghanistan, and the United States does have a right to detain combatants in a war, but they have to be treated as prisoners of war under the Geneva Conventions. This prohibits coercive interrogations. And no matter what label was applied to those picked up—POW or not—abuse; cruel, inhuman, and degrading treatment; and, of course, torture are all outlawed. The United States would have had the right to set up a POW camp, and that camp could have been in Guantánamo, but a POW camp is quite different from the lawless interrogation prison that Guantánamo became.

Ray: The Bush administration claimed that none of those picked up were POWs and that the Geneva Conventions had no application to the detainees. Is that claim correct?

Ratner: Absolutely not. The United States was at war with the nation of Afghanistan, which, like the United States, is a country that was and is a signatory to the Geneva Conventions. The Conventions state that they apply to an "armed conflict" between "two or more parties" to the conventions, so there should have been no question of their application to that war.

The Geneva Conventions are quite specific: those captured or detained in a war are protected by the conventions and should be treated as prisoners of war. If there is any doubt as to whether they are POWs, there is a special hearing procedure in which a "competent tribunal" makes an individualized determination as to whether a detained person is a POW. Until that tribunal meets and makes a decision, a detained person must be treated as a POW (see Appendix One: Documents). The United States, in fact, has a set of regulations that details the procedures before these "competent tribunals," and the United States has used them thousands of times in prior wars. But the administration refused to do so in this war.

If a hearing finds that a detainee is not a POW, he is then considered a civilian and he is protected by a different part of the conventions. Such a finding might mean that he had no right to take up weapons and kill enemy soldiers—a right given to the members of a country's military—and he could then be prosecuted for murder. Or the hearing might determine that a person is neither a POW nor a civilian who took up weapons, but was, in fact, taken prisoner by mistake. In that case he should be released. These hearings are crucial, particularly in a war where the United States claims the enemy soldiers did not wear uniforms; mistakes are inevitable in such circumstances and the need for hearings all the more pressing.

The key point here is that *everyone* picked up in a war is protected by the Geneva Conventions. No one is outside the law. No one can be treated arbitrarily at the discretion of his captors.

The End of the Rule of Law

Ray: In May 2004, the press obtained and made public a memo
dated January 25, 2002, from Counsel to the President Alberto
R. Gonzales, to the president, as well as a reply dated January 26,
2002, from Secretary of State Colin Powell to Gonzales,
regarding the application of the Geneva Conventions (see
Appendix One: Documents). What do these memos say about
the law that should be applied to those detained?

Ratner: The Gonzales memo is the beginning of the end of the
rule of law with regard to treatment of the Guantánamo prisoners. It openly recommends not applying the Geneva
Conventions to the Taliban and al Qaeda.

    The memo begins by saying that the president has the con-
stitutional authority to decide not to apply the Geneva
Conventions, which is an assumption that I reject. The conventions, ratified by the Senate, are the supreme law of the United
States under the Constitution and cannot simply be discarded
by the president acting alone.

    Gonzales gives three primary reasons for not wanting to
apply the conventions. First, a finding that they do not apply
"eliminates any argument regarding the need for case-by-case
determinations of POW status." Of course, case-by-case determinations are the very essence of the conventions and are
essential to individualized treatment required by law.

    Second, the war on terror "renders obsolete Geneva's strict
limitations on questioning of enemy combatants." In other
words, the conventions interfere with interrogation.

    And third, not applying the Geneva Conventions "substan-
tially reduces the threat of domestic criminal prosecution [of
administration officials] under the War Crimes Act (18 U.S.C.
2441)." That statute makes criminal grave breaches of the
Geneva Conventions whether or not the detainee is a POW.

Grave breaches include, as Gonzales points out, "outrages upon personal dignity" and "inhuman treatment." As he says, "it is difficult to predict the motives of prosecutors and independent counsel…in the future."

It seems obvious that, as early as January 2002, the Bush administration was planning on using (or had already used) interrogation techniques that it thought might constitute "inhuman treatment" and violate the conventions, thereby opening itself up to criminal prosecutions. Gonzales concluded that a presidential determination not to apply the conventions "would provide a solid defense to any future prosecutions."

Powell's reply memo strongly favors treatment of all detainees under the Geneva Conventions. He says the United States has never determined that the conventions do not apply in armed conflicts with U.S. forces, and that following the conventions would aid U.S. prisoners in being treated as POWs when captured, reduce legal challenges to the detentions, "present a positive international posture," and "preserve U.S. credibility and moral authority."

Clearly, Secretary Powell's advice was not followed; Abu Ghraib says it all.

Ray: Assuming the United States had followed the Geneva Conventions, what should have happened to the POWs?

Ratner: As I said earlier, POWs must be held in a POW camp, not a jail, and the level of restrictions imposed must be determined on an individual basis. POWs have a number of rights: they need only give identifying information (they can give more, but cannot be coerced into doing so), they must be released at the end of the conflict (in this case, the war with Afghanistan), and if they are tried for war crimes, they must be tried by the same system of courts as our own soldiers.

Those who are not found to be POWs can be released if

innocent, can be held in secure situations if "engaged in activities hostile to the security of the state," and can be interrogated and tried for war crimes if appropriate.

Ray: Almost two years ago, there were news reports that it was likely a large number of the prisoners at Guantánamo were not involved in terrorism. What does this say about U.S. policy?

Ratner: It shows that there should have been hearings right away. Even then it was apparent that many of the people in Guantánamo were innocent of any crime. A *Los Angeles Times* article said that, according to classified material, as many as 10 percent of the Guantánamo prisoners were "taxi drivers, farmers, cobblers, and laborers"; that some were "low-level figures conscripted by the Taliban in the weeks before the collapse of the ruling Afghanistan regime"; and that none of the sixty or so people discussed in the article met the criteria for being sent to Guantánamo.

And I think the 10 percent figure is a gross underestimate. Of the 147 prisoners who had been released two years later, only 13 were then sent to jails. The other 134 were guilty of absolutely nothing. That is already more than 10 percent of all the prisoners. It is certainly conceivable that the majority, perhaps a substantial majority, of the people in Guantánamo had nothing to do with any kind of terrorism.

Ray: In early March 2004, five British citizens were released from Guantánamo after two and a half years and sent to England. When they arrived, one was released immediately, and the other four were held for questioning for a day and then also released unconditionally. What does this tell us?

Ratner: It is truly remarkable. Almost as soon as they hit the soil in England, they were released. Two of those released were my clients, and negotiations were taking place between the

Americans and the British from the beginning, two and a half years earlier.

Again, this shows that had the United States obeyed the law to begin with, which is to say given people hearings immediately upon taking them captive—given them any rights at all—these people would have been released immediately. The United States simply kept innocent people in jail in a fashion that is completely outside the law. You can be sure these five Britishers were not guilty of anything at all, or the British would have put them on trial.

And this is not just about the loss of years of these people's lives, or about whatever brutalities they may have undergone while they were in custody. Think of what it says about everyone else who is still in Guantánamo. The United States has released a few of the many hundreds of people there, but many of the detained prisoners in Guantánamo, like those Britishers, may be innocent of any crime whatsoever.

Rule by Executive Fiat

Ray: President Bush claimed he was applying the Geneva Conventions to the Taliban, but not to al Qaeda. Is this so, and what does it mean?

Ratner: The president did say that in February 2002, but he went on to say that although the conventions applied to the Taliban, they would not be treated as POWs. So they were given no real status under the conventions and no real rights. It was completely illegal.

As to individuals picked up in Afghanistan, Pakistan, and other parts of the world because of an alleged relationship to terrorism or al Qaeda, he did say the conventions did not govern their treatment. On this point, as to those picked up outside the war zone, he may have been technically correct; the Geneva Conventions and the laws of war really apply only to conflicts between states and to civil wars. Al Qaeda and other alleged international terrorists unconnected with the war would not be governed by these rules.

But if the conventions and the laws of war do not apply to alleged terrorists, this does not mean that no law applies to their treatment. Those individuals should have been protected by the set of laws that applies outside of war, a body of law called human rights law, of which criminal law is a branch. Under that set of laws, those detained have a right to an almost immediate hearing before a court, the right to a lawyer, and the right to be charged with a crime. But, of course, the Bush administration did not give anyone the normal rights that apply to those detained outside of war. Yet, while the administration acted as if the "war on terrorism" was a traditional type of war, they would not apply the Geneva Conventions that apply to such war.

Ray: What did this Bush decision mean in practice?

Ratner: Once the president made a decision that no Taliban soldier was in reality protected by the conventions, and that no individual allegedly involved with terrorism or al Qaeda was protected by the conventions or by any other laws, the situation of those detained by the United States around the world became lawless. The treatment of the detainees was left up to the sole discretion of government officials—a lawless situation.

Ray: But isn't the United States saying that the laws of war apply to those it picked up in Afghanistan, Pakistan, and elsewhere?

Ratner: The president is claiming that the laws of war apply to all those at Guantánamo, all those picked up in the so-called war on terror. But the president is using the laws of war selectively, picking and choosing them as he wants.

There are only two legal systems that apply in dealing with arrests, captures, and detentions: criminal law/ human rights law or the laws of war (sometimes called humanitarian law). But the United States has set up a third system that depends entirely on its own discretion and its own notion of the laws of war.

Ray: Under what legal theory was this done?
Ratner: That's just it: there is none. This is not authorized by law, not by treaty, and not by customary international law. The laws of war only apply to armed conflicts between two states or to a civil war. When the United States and Germany were at war in World War II, the laws of war applied, and soldiers of one side captured on the battlefield by soldiers of the other side were detained as prisoners of war in prisoner of war camps. And they could be—and were—held in those camps until the war was over. That is where the laws of war apply. This is, of course, what should have been done with the Taliban but was not.

Until now this doctrine has never been applied to conflicts that were not between internationally recognized states or civil wars. It has not been applied to terrorism—not in England, not in Ireland, not in Germany during the Baader-Meinhof attacks. If some fundamentalist or separatist group bombs a building, the persons arrested and charged are not treated under the laws of war; they are treated under criminal law.

But now the United States has said that the laws of war apply to al Qaeda, to al Qaeda supporters, and to virtually anyone they say is an international terrorist. Why? Because, as presidential counselor Gonzales admitted, the administration wants to "use every tool and weapon—including the advantages presented by the laws of war—to win the war." The laws of war are more flexible than criminal law; if you pick up a soldier, you can simply detain that solder until the end of the war, with no charges, no lawyers, no trial. And if that war is endless, the detentions are endless, or so the administration says.

Ray: How did they justify this use of the laws of war?

Ratner: They justified this in part by arguing that the congressional resolution authorizing the president to use force against those responsible for 9/11 turned the situation into a war. But calling it a war against terrorism, or even authorizing military force to capture alleged terrorists, does not make it a war between nation states or a civil war. It is still an international law enforcement action to which normal criminal law applies.

Ray: Is the administration actually applying the laws of war to those at Guantánamo?

Ratner: In fact, it doesn't really want to apply the laws of war across the board. It wants to pick and choose, applying the draconian aspects of those laws without granting any of the rights they give to those captured. The United States will not call the people held at Guantánamo prisoners of war, or even prisoners, the official designation being "detained personnel," or simply detainees. The Pentagon has made up a new term: "enemy combatant." The entire world is a battlefield, they argue, and all people picked up in that battlefield are enemy combatants because they are fighting against the United States. Therefore, they can be held beyond the end of the war in Afghanistan, beyond the end of the war in Iraq, until the end of the war on terrorism. And that, Secretary Rumsfeld and other officials say, could be fifty years or more down the road.

This is a totalitarian system in which there are no checks and balances on the executive. The president can do whatever he wants, acting as dictator. In this system the courts have no independent function and can't protect anybody's rights. The

Bush administration has tried to justify this system in the Supreme Court, arguing that it must have full control without "judicial micro-managing." In essence, the president claims he can order the indefinite detention of noncitizens simply because he says so, and no court can review his decision.

The president has ordered people captured or detained from all over the world—Afghanistan, Pakistan, Africa, the Philippines, Yugoslavia. He has had them put on airplanes and taken them to Guantánamo, a jurisdiction he claims is a law-free zone where prisoners have no right to lawyers and no right to be charged. He detains them as long as he wants and then says that no court can examine what he is doing and that the prisoners have no right to file writs of habeas corpus in U.S. courts.

Then, when it was decided to try some of the prisoners at Guantánamo, while others languished in prison, the president set up a tribunal of his own to try them, with all of its members appointed by him or by the Pentagon and with Rumsfeld et al. having the right to overrule any decisions they don't like. This is no justice at all.

Ray: Under the traditional rules of war, does one have the right to interrogate prisoners constantly, as the United States admits it is doing in Guantánamo and elsewhere?

Ratner: The Germans did that during World War II. They ran detention centers that were called interrogation camps, not prisoner of war camps. The 1949 Geneva Conventions outlawed interrogation camps and required that such prisoners be treated as POWs. What we have in Guantánamo today is an illegal interrogation camp, an offshore interrogation camp.

The administration simply declares that its prisoners are not prisoners of war, they are enemy combatants, and despite the 1949 conventions, they will not be treated as POWs. There is no legal justification for what the United States is doing, no matter what you call the prisoners. The U.S. inquisitors are not just asking for name, rank, and serial number: they are interrogating people morning, noon, and night. Whether you call it torture; cruel, inhuman, and degrading treatment; or stress and duress, it is a violation of international law.

Ray: Are there other ways the government can deal with those it claims are dangerous suspects? What, in your view, should have happened?

Ratner: The government should have treated 9/11 as a criminal act and not as an act of war. It was not the act of a nation-state; it was the act of a band of criminals or terrorists who wanted to attack the United States. But the Bush administration immediately decided to treat it as an act of war and not simply as an international law enforcement matter. It began to assume war powers, commander-in-chief powers, to override the U.S. Constitution, the court system, Congress, and fundamental aspects of treaties and international human rights law. By labeling it a war, the president had the opportunity to assume huge powers.

Combatants picked up on the battlefield in Afghanistan should have been treated as POWs and held in POW camps, not coercively interrogated, and released at the close of that war. Alleged terrorists should have been treated the way alleged criminals are treated. They are arrested, incarcerated, and given a court hearing, with a lawyer. The court decides whether there is sufficient evidence to hold them in prison and bring them to trial. But the United States has refused to do that.

Ray: As you have said, the administration uses the term enemy combatants to describe those at Guantánamo. What does that term really mean? Where does it come from?

Ratner: In its use of the term enemy combatants and in its discussion of the treatment of people under the laws of war, the government bases much of its argument on a famous World War II case called *Ex Parte Quirin*. The *Quirin* case concerned German saboteurs who snuck into the United States supposedly to commit acts of sabotage. They were tried before a military tribunal and convicted, some of them were executed immediately; others were released at the end of the war. This case saw the first real use of the term "unlawful combatant."

But, notwithstanding the similarity of the terms, the *Quirin* case shouldn't apply to the Guantánamo prisoners. *Quirin* involved a declared war between two nation-states, and the defendants were spies or saboteurs working directly for the German enemy. But even those people got a trial—not one whose procedures would be acceptable today, but at least a trial. They were not simply detained forever without any hearing. So the case should not provide any authority for the administration to hold people who are not connected with a nation-state indefinitely without a trial. To the extent some of those in Guantánamo are from the Taliban army, they should be treated as POWs and not as enemy combatants, a legally meaningless term. This is a broad designation the Bush administration is employing to make it appear that those it is detaining in Guantánamo and elsewhere can be held indefinitely and without rights.

Ray: Is there any basis at all for the administration's claim that it can label those at Guantánamo enemy combatants?

Ratner: The point is that the label does not have any legal significance. Its obvious and only real meaning is the dictionary meaning—a person from another nation who has taken up arms, in this case against the United States. The Bush administration is using this term to refer to alleged terrorists who do not belong to a nation-state and who should be tried under criminal law. Those detainees are not enemy combatants but alleged terrorist suspects.

The administration is using the term enemy combatants for combatants captured in Afghanistan and Iraq who should be classified as prisoners of war. That is what the Geneva Conventions require and that is what the administration is ignoring. Enemy combatant is sort of a catchall term, to which no status or rights apply under international or domestic law and which the administration thus believes it can use to treat people as it wants.

This use of the term has been widely condemned. In 2002, for example, the Inter-American Commission on Human Rights of the Organization of American States said that all those at Guantánamo had to have immediate hearings to determine their status. The administration ignored that ruling.

The administration has also used the term enemy combatant to deny the right to a hearing to those at Guantánamo. In a war, the administration claims, one can hold captured soldiers as POWs until the end of the war and no hearings are required. But conventional wars have an end. Here, the administration claims it can hold detainees forever, without the protections that apply to POWs under the Geneva Conventions.

The prisoners in Guantánamo deserve some kind of hearing, rather than indefinite detention. Of course, Rumsfeld says that prisoners can be kept in Guantánamo even after they have been tried by one of the military tribunals. And if they are convicted and serve a sentence, they can still be kept in Guantánamo after that, until he or the president determines they are not a danger to the security of the United States.

Ray: Has there been litigation outside the United States, other than the decision of the Inter-American Commission on Human Rights of the Organization of American States?

Ratner: A British court in the *Abassi* case said that the prisoners at Guantánamo were in a "legal black hole," that they had no rights under the system the United States was using, and urged the United States—over which the British court conceded it had no jurisdiction—to grant the prisoners hearings.

Ray: Do these decisions have any weight with U.S. courts?

Ratner: Courts can look to these decisions, consider their reasoning, and use it in thinking about their decisions in a case—or at least they should do so.

Ray: Isn't the administration orchestrating a campaign to try to intimidate federal judges, including the Supreme Court, from citing or considering foreign court decisions such as these, or even foreign opinion?

Ratner: Yes, and a Sense of the House Resolution to this effect has been introduced in the House of Representatives.

Ray: Did the Red Cross give an opinion about the application of the Geneva Conventions to Guantánamo?

Ratner: Yes. The Red Cross rarely goes public, but it did on this issue. Of the Guantánamo detainees picked up in the war zone the Red Cross said, "They were captured in combat [and] we consider them prisoners of war."

Ray: Shortly after 9/11, the president issued a military order that provided for detentions of noncitizens without trial. What is this order and is that the order under which prisoners of Guantánamo are currently being detained?

Ratner: Initially, it was assumed that most of those captured and detained at Guantánamo were detained under the president's Military Order No. 1 (see Appendix One: Documents). But in fact, it later turned out that, according to the Bush administration, most were not detained under the Order, but under the president's powers as commander in chief.

Nonetheless, Military Order No. 1 was a shock. The president, without congressional authority, issued it on November 13, 2001. It was an action taken by President Bush as commander in chief. The order was extraordinary in that it defined people whom the president could detain at will, simply by designating any noncitizen an alleged international terrorist or someone associated with international terrorists, with no legal safeguards and no court orders, nothing but a note from the president to the secretary of defense to detain someone, for as long as the president wants, with no way to appeal such a designation.

The president decided that he was no longer running the country as a civilian president. He issued a military order giving himself the power to run the country as a general. Under the order he claimed the absolute power to arrest noncitizens anywhere in the world, even in the Unites States, and hold them indefinitely and without charges or a lawyer until the so-called war on terror was over, which could be fifty years or forever.

Military Order No. 1 also set up a system of military tribunals to try alleged terrorists, a system heavily slanted toward conviction. Virtually all noncitizens, everywhere in the world, became subject to the whim of the U.S. executive branch if, in the president's sole discretion, they fit into one of three categories: alleged members of al Qaeda; anyone who harbors alleged members of al Qaeda, whatever "harboring" means; and most frighteningly, anybody alleged to be involved in international terrorism, whatever "involved" means and whatever "international terrorism" means. This is an administration filled with people who considered members of the African National Congress and of most other national liberation movements of the last few decades as international terrorists.

Ray: How can it be that a presidential order allowing for indefinite detention was issued with so little outcry or even public discussion of that concept?

Ratner: As it happened, even though Military Order No. 1 allowed for indefinite detention, it wasn't seen that way when it came out; it was looked at as an order setting up tribunals. It did outline the basics procedures for those tribunals, which were appalling, and there was some discussion of and opposition to that.

The tribunals were going to be held outside the United States, totally in secret, with military officers as judges. The prosecution was going to be allowed to bring in any kind of evidence, including hearsay evidence. And they allowed the imposition of the death penalty by a majority vote of the judges. So there was initially some protest about the procedures, both within the United States and around the world.

The order contains a draconian detention policy. It says the secretary of defense shall detain such people as the president designates, and that *if* they are tried, certain procedures will apply. But it does not say they ever actually *have to be* tried.

Enemy Combatants

Ray: If Military Order No. 1 is not the legal justification for most of the detentions at Guantánamo, under what authority are prisoners being held?

Ratner: The Bush administration claimed, under the president's constitutional commander-in-chief powers in fighting "the war on terrorism," unilateral authority to arrest virtually anyone, anywhere, noncitizen or citizen, even in the United States, if he deemed them an enemy combatant. And this was not only the basis for most of the detentions of noncitizens at Guantánamo, but also the president's claimed basis for the detentions in military brigs in the United States of American citizens José Padilla and Yaser Esam Hamdi.

In some ways this is worse than detention under the Military Order; at least under the Order a detainee must arguably fit within one of the three categories referred to above. Under these claimed commander-in-chief powers the president can and presumably does designate people enemy combatants and detain them for whatever reason he wants. When the president's counsel, Alberto Gonzales, described this sweeping power the president now claims, in a speech to the American Bar Association, he said that the "determination that an individual is an enemy combatant is a quintessentially military judgment" to which the courts, if they inquire at all, must give "great deference."

In any event, when the administration initially issued Military Order No. 1, it was thinking of enemy combatants as noncitizens. It thought of terrorists as a group as noncitizens and realized there would be less opposition to going after them with this Military Order.

And in either type of detention—whether under the Military Order or the commander-in-chief powers—there are no charges and prisoners have no lawyers, no family visits, no court review, no rights to anything, and no right to release until the mythical end of the "war on terror." It is truly terrifying. If the Bush administration argument is accepted, it can detain people forever and torture them, and there is nothing any court can do about it.

Ray: In fact, a few of the people swept up in these operations were indeed U.S. citizens. Are there differences between their treatment and the treatment of the noncitizens in Guantánamo?

Ratner: One of the people supposedly picked up on a battlefield in Afghanistan and taken to Guantánamo, Yaser Esam Hamdi, turned out to be a U.S. citizen. So, demonstrating their discrimination against noncitizens, they took Hamdi to a brig in South Carolina, to conditions that might be marginally better than in Guantánamo.

For Hamdi, at least, as a U.S. citizen held in the United States, the courthouse doors were not altogether closed as they were for the noncitizens at Guantánamo. Hamdi could go to court, and the government had to affirm that it picked him up on the battlefield and classified him as an enemy combatant. However, he is still not allowed to have a lawyer to contest his detention, to challenge the hearsay allegations in the government's affidavit, to call witnesses. He may be an American citizen, but he could still sit forever in a brig in South Carolina, merely on the say-so of some low government official, unless, of course, his position is upheld in the Supreme Court.

Later, another U.S. citizen, Jose Padilla, was also designated as an enemy combatant. His is an even more extreme case of the misuse of military law or the laws of war, detaining someone who should have been brought before a criminal court, if he was to be held at all.

He was not picked up on the battlefield, not even arrested in a foreign country. The FBI arrested him as he got off a plane in Chicago. First, he was held as a material witness, someone whose testimony the government might want for a grand jury. But then the president classified him as an enemy combatant, allegedly because Padilla was investigating the use of a "dirty bomb" somewhere in the United States. Of course, we have no idea if they have any evidence of this, and why, if they do, they didn't just bring him to trial for it.

But they didn't indict him and try him. Instead, they swept him from the jail where he was sitting as a material witness, took him to South Carolina, and put him in a Navy brig without any attorney. Imagine, the government merely alleged that a U.S. citizen was involved in some plot and was therefore an enemy combatant who could be locked up forever. As with Hamdi, the government justified his detention solely on the basis of an affidavit, which could not be contested.

After two years, the government allowed Hamdi and Padilla to see attorneys, but only because these cases reached the Supreme Court. Even so, the attorneys were kept in a separate room and their conversations with their clients were videotaped. And the government has not conceded that the attorneys can use any of the information they might have been given to defend their clients. Of course, it was difficult, if not impossible, for the attorneys to discuss the cases with their clients when they finally met; the government was listening.

Ray: What about John Walker Lindh? He wasn't dealt with as an enemy combatant, was he?

Ratner: No, he wasn't. John Walker Lindh, a U.S. citizen, the so-called American Taliban, was picked up on the battlefield in Afghanistan, probably by the Northern Alliance, and then turned over to the Americans after being kept in a metal container for two days, strapped to a gurney, naked and blindfolded, in extreme heat. These conditions constitute, in my view, unlawful physical torture.

He was then turned over to the Americans. And because he was an American citizen from a privileged background, and because, I think, they were nervous about what had been done to him, they indicted him, gave him all his rights to counsel, and intended to go forward with a normal criminal trial. In the end he made a deal and pleaded guilty.

Lindh was facing a possible life sentence, or even the death penalty. It is possible that the government threatened that unless he pleaded guilty, it would simply classify him as an enemy combatant, forgo any trial, and hold him indefinitely.

This is apparently what occurred with a group of young men arrested in Buffalo, New York, as alleged conspirators in a "sleeper cell." They all pleaded guilty because of the threat that they would be charged as enemy combatants and incarcerated indefinitely.

CHAPTER TWO

ABUSE AND TORTURE

The United Nations Convention Against Torture

Ray: There have been allegations from the very beginning that prisoners at Guantánamo were being tortured or abused, and a number of those who have been released described the treatment they received there as torture or abuse. What is happening there? Is torture allowed under international law? Is abusive conduct permitted?

Ratner: Torture has been prohibited for many, many years. The key document today that prohibits torture is the United Nations Convention Against Torture, an international treaty that almost every country in the world, including the United States, has ratified (see Appendix One: Documents). The Convention Against Torture says that under no circumstances can torture be used: it is an international crime, and every country in the world must pass legislation to make it a crime. The United States has made it a crime even if it occurs abroad. Not only torture but other forms of abuse are prohibited by the Convention Against Torture: cruel, inhuman, and degrading treatment (conduct that is severe, but not so severe as to amount to torture) is also prohibited. A stress position, for example, such as forced standing for a number of hours, might not be torture but is still prohibited.

The Convention Against Torture also establishes what is called *universal jurisdiction* for cases of torture. This means that if a person is accused of torture and flees to or is present in another country, that country, if it signed the convention, has an absolute obligation to arrest that person, investigate, and either try him for torture or extradite him to the country from which he fled.

So, for example, if an American citizen engaged in torture anywhere in the world and was later found in France, let's say, that person could be arrested in France and either tried for torture there or extradited to the place of the torture for trial. To the extent U.S. officials were or are involved in torture in Guantánamo or elsewhere, they should be careful about the countries in which they travel.

In fact, the prohibition against torture is the most fundamental international human rights prohibition, one that virtually all the nations of the world had agreed upon long before it was fully codified in the Convention.

Torture is also prohibited by customary international law—that is law that has arisen by the practices of nations. It is an absolute prohibition: under no circumstance can you torture anybody, ever. It has taken hundreds of years for this absolute prohibition to evolve into universally accepted law, but it is now an integral part of both treaty law and customary international law. The prohibition applies whether or not one is protected by the Geneva Conventions, which also prohibit torture and inhuman treatment of anyone, POW or not, who is in the custody of a government as a result of a war (see Appendix One: Documents).

Ray: Is there any argument that can be made that torture and similar abuses are lawful if not used against prisoners of war but against unlawful combatants?

Ratner: Absolutely not. The Convention Against Torture applies to every human being. The Geneva Conventions apply to every type of combatant in a war. Even if one argues that al Qaeda suspects are not governed by the Geneva Conventions, the Convention Against Torture and other human rights treaties ratified by the United States prohibit torture as well as other cruel, inhuman, and degrading treatment.

Nor does the Convention Against Torture permit any excuses for torture. Article 2 says that "no exceptional circumstances whatsoever"—whether a state of war or a threat of war, political instability, or any other public emergency—may be evoked as a justification of torture. It goes on to say that an order from a superior officer or a public authority may not be invoked as a justification for torture. That is an illegal order, and you can be punished as a criminal for carrying it out.

The convention is crystal clear: under no circumstances can you torture people, whatever you call them, whether illegal combatants, enemy combatants, murderers, killers. You cannot torture anybody ever; it's an absolute prohibition.

So classifying these people as threats to the United States has nothing to do with how you must treat them. They still have to be treated humanely, and humane treatment does not include torture.

In addition, torture committed by U.S. soldiers or private contractors acting under U.S. authority is a violation of federal law, punishable by the death penalty if the death of a prisoner results from the torture. Another federal statute criminalizes any grave breach of the Geneva Conventions—including torture, willful killing, inhuman treatment, and causing great suffering to those in custody—as a war crime. Furthermore, a special statute criminalizes such conduct if carried out by so-called private contractors working with the U.S. military.

Ray: How is torture defined?
Ratner: The Convention Against Torture defines torture as "any

act by which severe pain or suffering, whether physical or mental, is intentionally inflicted on a person" by a public or state official for any of a variety of reasons: punishment, getting information, and similar kinds of things. Also included in the definition of torture is the use of mind-altering drugs. The definition used in U.S. law is quite similar.

In other words, if a government official, whether a soldier, doctor, intelligence agent, military policeman, or contract interrogator, inflicts severe mental or physical pain on a detainee, that is considered torture. Something that is not considered sufficiently severe to be torture may fall into that lesser category called cruel, inhuman, and degrading treatment.

For example, during the 1970s the British prison authorities forced prisoners from the Irish Republican Army to stand hooded for long periods of time against a wall, six or eight hours at a stretch. While that was not considered torture, it was considered cruel, inhuman, and degrading treatment, and was considered illegal.

Ray: Since 9/11, there have been some arguments made that torture may be necessary to get information about the next terrorist attack. While you say that the Convention Against Torture allows no such exception, don't these developments have some effect on the arguments that the prohibition on torture and similar conduct should be loosened?

Ratner: Initially, the most common hypothetical scenario was the capture of a person who knew the whereabouts of a nuclear bomb hidden in the middle of Manhattan, attached to a timer. The argument was that it was justified—more than that, it was just common sense—to torture that person until he revealed the location of the bomb, so it could be disarmed and the innocent residents of Manhattan saved. Most of the initial discussion actually centered on the conflict in Israel and the early cases of suicide bombers.

As revelations about the use of stress and duress and torture in U.S. detention camps have come out, a number of critics have been quick to excuse and to defend, to try to come up with a system that authorizes or justifies such tactics. One of the most ubiquitous is Alan Dershowitz, who says, look, if they are going to use torture anyway, why don't we have a system, where you have to go to a court and get a warrant to be allowed to torture someone. Then, he says, we could control its use.

To me, this is an incredibly outrageous position, particularly for someone who considers himself a civil rights lawyer. It ignores the hundreds and hundreds of years during which civilizations have finally determined and agreed that torture is not civilized, in any circumstances. And it has many dangerous implications in situations less blatant than outright torture. Should we have the government go to a court to ask for permission to use stress and duress or sleep deprivation or dangerous drugs, or to keep a prisoner naked and with limited food? Is that the kind of society we want to live in?

Another critical aspect about torture is that, as many law enforcement officials acknowledge, you are not getting information that is accurate. You are potentially lining up and torturing a lot of innocent people who have nothing to do with anything and no information.

It is also counterproductive to treat people the way the United States does in Guantánamo or Bagram or Abu Ghraib if you want people to cooperate in the war on terrorism. Muslims and people of Arab ethnicity are angry and inflamed by what is being done to their people. They are not going to cooperate; worse, they are going to turn against you.

So even from a pragmatic point of view, there is a strong basis for opposing torture under any circumstance. Apart from its ineffectiveness and illegality, torture is one of the cruelest, and most dangerous things that the United States can be doing.

The claim that torture should somehow be justified is really an attack on the very dignity of humanity. It sinks us all to an inhuman and uncivilized level. It debases the victim and the torturer. In the end, torture destroys everything we value as human beings.

The Trip to Guantánamo

Ray: Although there are still thousands of prisoners being held in Afghanistan, many were transported to Guantánamo. Is there any cause for concern regarding the journey itself?

Ratner: Yes, a lot could happen and has happened along that route, from capture by warlords fighting against the Taliban and ultimately allied to the United States, to detention by U.S. troops in Kandahar or Bagram, and then in Guantánamo. A lot of the people picked up by warlords of the Northern Alliance were kept in metal shipping containers, so tightly packed that they had to ball themselves up, and the heat was unbearable. According to some detainees who were held in the containers and eventually released from Guantánamo, only a small number, thirty to fifty people in a container filled with three to four hundred people survived. And some of those released said that the Americans were in on this, that the Americans were shining lights on the containers. The people inside were suffocating, so the Northern Alliance soldiers shot holes into the containers, killing some of the prisoners inside.

So the first way they "winnowed down" the numbers, as Rumsfeld put it, was by killing them. And the survivors were turned over to the United States and sent to Bagram and Kandahar, where they were subject to very heavy measures and intense interrogation.

Ray: Were people physically abused when in U.S. custody in Afghanistan?

Ratner: Yes, in both Kandahar and Bagram prisoners were beaten, shackled all the time, forced to lie flat on the floor, kicked, pushed down into the ground, given almost nothing to eat, and kept on their knees for sixteen hours at a time. This amounts in my view to cruel, inhuman, and degrading treatment, and seems to fit the definition of torture under the Convention Against Torture. It is a violation of the Geneva Conventions as well. Things were so bad at Bagram that it became known to many as the torture chamber of the United States.

After a month in Kandahar some of the prisoners were dressed in orange jumpsuits, put into chains that tied their legs, arms, and waists together, and flown to Guantánamo. Wearing blacked out goggles and ear coverings, they were shackled and chained flat against the floor in a transport plane for twenty-four hours. They didn't know where they were going. They weren't allowed to get up to go to the bathroom. After a few hours they were lying on the floor in their own urine and feces.

The photographed arrival of the Guantánamo prisoners created one of the more enduring images of the U.S. war on terror. The Muslim world and others were shocked when they saw crew-cut marines standing over a row of kneeling, shackled, goggled Muslim men in the Cuban sun. It became an iconic image of all that the United States was doing wrong to the Muslim world.

The British prisoners whom we represent spent the next two years under extremely high-security imprisonment at Guantánamo. First, they were detained at Camp X-Ray in dog-run-like cages, exposed to the elements and at the mercy of the Immediate Reaction Force (IRF), which would go into the cages and beat people up, a process that came to be called "IRFing." Some of these beatings were taped and have recently been requested by one of the congressional committees involved in the investigation. They may turn out to be important evidence of abuse and torture, if the most damaging evidence implicating these IRF squads has not already been destroyed by the military.

In the middle of 2002 the cells of those initially imprisoned in the dog-run cells were upgraded and a number of prisoners, including our clients, were transferred from Camp X-Ray to Camp Delta. These prisoners were still in cage-like cells, three sides of which were chain link. Prisoners had their hair shaved off; their toilets were holes in the floor; they had to stoop to get water; and guards, female and male, walked by them twice every minute, so they had absolutely no privacy. The detainees were deprived of the most basic utensils for human care. And they underwent scores and scores of additional interrogations under coercive conditions. Some of these may have been videotaped as well. It was during this process that some of the released British detainees made false confessions.

Ray: How are the Guantánamo camps set up?

Ratner: There is a series of cell blocks, one after the other, just like storage facilities. Within Camp Delta there are levels one through four.

Within each camp there are different levels, depending on how much you've cooperated. Level one is for the cooperators, levels two through four for the people who don't cooperate. Then there is level four-minus. Once you get into level four-minus, from what I understand, you're essentially in isolation, with no utensils, maybe a little bit of cloth or something to sleep on, but really very, very harsh conditions.

There is another camp, Camp Echo, which is considered solitary, and is primarily for those people who are going to face commissions. There may also be people there whom the captors consider problems.

They have built two new camps, Romeo and Tango, "R&T,"

which are going to be worse than the others: total isolation camps. In these camps the detainees can be put in stripped, and after a few days given shorts—that is all they are given to wear—which only go down to about half a foot above the knee. These are for Muslim men who pray four or five times a day, men whose knees are supposed to be covered. When they sit and pray in these shorts, anyone can look into the pants and see their genitals. This is obviously meant to embarrass them and tear down the human personality of the people involved.

Ray: But the Pentagon claims it is treating the prisoners at Guantánamo well, that it is a model institution, that it is respecting the prisoners' religion, providing Muslims with prayer rugs, the Koran, and "culturally appropriate meals."

Ratner: This is not at all true. There are many different levels to consider in the abuses suffered there. First, there is a psychological level. People, as far we know, have been (and are still being) rounded up and taken to Guantánamo from all over the Islamic world, where they are put into wire-mesh cages for observation. They are isolated from each other and repeatedly taken into separate interrogation booths—trailers, really.

A critical psychological issue is that these people have no idea if or when they are ever getting out. For all they know, each time they are taken out of their cells they may well be put up against a wall and shot.

Ray: I read reports a year or so ago that the camp commander at the time, Major General Geoffrey Miller, floated a rumor in the media and also let it become known around the camp that the new, hard-walled prison Halliburton was building—Camp Echo—was to be a death row prison, with its own execution chamber.

Ratner: Yes, and this just reinforced the belief in the prisoners' minds that Guantánamo was the end of the line, a death camp.

The Red Cross has said one of the most psychologically devastating things happening to people in Guantánamo is the notion that they have reached a dead end, that there is no way out. The psychological harm is horrendous. In fact, one of the threats employed to make prisoners in Iraq talk, even after they had been subjected to abuse and torture, was to threaten them with going to Guantánamo, because everyone understood that there was little or no chance of ever getting out of there.

About one in five of the prisoners have been put on antidepressants, psychotropics, and other drugs. In addition to hunger strikes, there have been more than thirty suicide attempts.

Guantánamo is like Dante's ninth circle of hell. The temperature is often 110 degrees Fahrenheit, and of course the prisoners have no such thing as air conditioning. The place is infested by scorpions and banana rats. The detainees sleep on concrete floors, with no mattresses; the toilet is a hole in the ground. It is a horrific situation from a physical, psychological, and legal point of view.

Ray: You mentioned that mental as well as physical torture is prohibited. Guantánamo has been referred to as an experimental laboratory in psychiatric detention. It has been suggested that the prisoners have become test subjects for developing methods of interrogation in order to track and classify Islamic societies.

Ratner: Yes. In fact, one interrogator who was interviewed on CBS television boasted that some of the prisoners "are being kept as a kind of al Qaeda database to be mined indefinitely by the interrogators." He also admitted, "It wouldn't be prudent to let any of them go if we thought they had any information of value."

Unfortunately, we have very limited information as to precisely what is happening at Guantánamo, and there will always be dangerously cynical arguments about whether certain conduct is literally torture or whether it is simply cruel, inhuman, and degrading treatment. But both are abhorrent and contrary to the Convention Against Torture and the Geneva Conventions.

We don't have any real observers in Guantánamo. The Red Cross goes there, but its people cannot examine the interrogation rooms, which are separate and secret. The Red Cross has made clear that their inability to speak publicly on this issue should not be taken to mean that torture is not happening there. In May 2004, it was reported that the Red Cross had issued a report on conditions at Guantánamo and furnished that report to the U.S. government. While Red Cross reports are not made public, some of the details have come out. These include stripping of inmates, short-shackling, and the use of medical information to coerce detainees into cooperating. These coercive techniques are precisely those that the released British clients have spoken about publicly for a few months.

The Red Cross publicly addressed the issue of mental torture at Guantánamo, without using the word torture. They say that what is happening to people's mental stability and mental health is extremely serious, and they have condemned it very strongly, pointing out that keeping people in a camp for two years with no rights, no lawyers, no charges, no sense at all of if or when they might be released, has caused a quantifiable deterioration in their mental health. One could certainly argue that that fits the definition in the Convention of severe mental pain or suffering.

We do know from a number of the people who have been released from Guantánamo that mental torture, the breaking down of the human spirit, is the norm there. This is an interrogation camp, and they are consciously trying to take away people's identities. Prisoners get toothbrushes, decent food, and other amenities only as a reward for cooperating.

Ray: But it is now abundantly clear that there is much more to their poor treatment than the withholding of amenities and the granting of rewards, isn't it?

Ratner: There is definitely physical brutality. There are squads of U.S. military personnel—the IRFs I mentioned earlier—who occasionally beat people up, sometimes quite severely. They have held back food from recalcitrant prisoners. There are reports that during interrogation, prisoners are forced to kneel, sometimes for hours while they are chained to a ring on the floor.

The sleep deprivation I mentioned earlier has been openly admitted and authorized in Guantánamo by the Pentagon. As a result of the Abu Ghraib scandal, the Pentagon has said it is banning the use of sleep deprivation in Iraq; it remains to be seen whether its use continues in Guantánamo.

The goal of breaking down people's will is to make them faceless, take away their culture, their religion, and their identities. The only chance they have to stop the endless interrogations is to cooperate. And the fact is that eventually many of the victims do cooperate, although cooperation may often lead to the signing of false confessions.

Interrogations

Ray: How intensive are the interrogations?

Ratner: The government has admitted that it conducts three hundred interrogations a week. In mid-2004, it had 2,800 soldiers and civilians (including interrogators) running a camp with somewhat more than seven hundred prisoners for two years. Some of the prisoners recently released from Guantánamo said they themselves had been interrogated as many as two hundred times, with all kinds of different techniques.

The United States is planning to use information gained during these interrogations in the military commissions. It is awful enough to try to gain intelligence for the so-called war on terror through torture and coercion, but to compound that by using coerced information in criminal proceedings is to double the outrage. These are obviously coerced statements and totally unreliable. After being held in isolation for two years, people will say anything, particularly if their next meal or the avoidance of coercive techniques depends on it.

Ray: Where do the interrogations take place and how are they done?

Ratner: The interrogations take place in special interrogation rooms where the Red Cross is not allowed. We've seen pictures; there's a metal chair and a steel ring on the floor. It reminds you of slave ships to see that metal ring on the floor. Some of the released prisoners said they were chained in what are called three-piece suits, which is a chain around the waist, shackled to another around the legs and still another around the arms. And then the prisoners are taken into the interrogation room. The chair in the photographs may be just for publicity purposes, to make it look like they get to sit. Detainees were chained flat on the floor, wrists onto that ring. Some said they were chained there for twelve hours, and others said they heard of people chained for sixteen hours at a time, not allowed to go to the bathroom, having to relieve themselves while they were chained there, which is incredibly embarrassing and humiliating. And those interrogation sessions would go on and on.

Various intelligence agencies interrogated detainees. For the United States these included the FBI, the CIA, and the Department of Defense. Interrogrations of British prisoners would include people from MI5, the British intelligence agency. People from Mossad, the Israeli intelligence agency, interviewed some Moroccans.

In the early days of the camp a loudspeaker would blare out the words, "Cooperate and you can go home," several times a day, spoken by the general or somebody else high up. And then another announcement followed, "A lot of people are leaving in the next few days. You can join them by cooperating." Another message was, "We know who is telling the truth and who is lying and we can tell. Tell the truth."

Ray: The former commander, Major General Miller, stated that three-quarters of the prisoners have been "very cooperative" as a result of his having instituted a rewards-and-punishment system. In this context, what does cooperation mean?

Ratner: It means telling the interrogators everything about your life, about all your acquaintances, anything they want to know about people back home, so they can also be rounded up and arrested. And it means confessing to whatever they want you to confess to. It means lying to them to avoid coercive punishments and to get yourself a McDonald's Happy Meal or a Twinkie or a toothbrush, or, more importantly, to get transferred to another part of the camp that is not so humiliating and degrading. The "intelligence" about terrorism and terrorists that is coming out of the Guantánamo interrogations is therefore basically garbage. It is simply not reliable. Confessions and denunciations obtained under these kinds of coercive conditions are useless, not just for a criminal trial but for getting any real intelligence that might actually protect the people of the world against terrorist attacks.

We see example after example of that in Guantánamo, where people have falsely confessed to knowledge about Osama bin Laden or to having been somewhere or done something, or have implicated others, all to get some kind of reward, even a pitiful Big Mac.

They are constantly getting people to nail one another. They will wear someone down until, when they ask for the

hundredth time "What do you know about Mr. X," he will
finally say, "Okay, he was with me at an Osama training camp."
And then they go to Mr. X and say, "Well, this guy says you
were with him at an Osama training camp, we have the evidence, you might as well confess."

Now, this prisoner has been totally incommunicado for two
years, under the thumb of a military that can feed him or not
feed him, keep the light on or not keep the light on, give him
exercise or not give him exercise, let him shower or not let him
shower, strip him or give him clothes, keep him in solitary or
not keep him in solitary, sometimes have him beaten up and
sometimes subject him to sleep deprivation. Eventually, he too
is going to say, "Yes, I was there with the other guy at the Osama
camp in Afghanistan." And there won't be a word of truth to it.

Ray: The United States claims that the detainees are getting good
medical care. What have you heard about this from your clients?

Ratner: The government brags that the prisoners are getting
better medical care than they got in Afghanistan or in Pakistan.
In fact, medical care, like meals, is withheld if you don't cooperate, according to some of those released. If you have some
kind of pain or you need some sort of medicine, they won't give
it to you unless you cooperate. They hold it out as a reward for
cooperation.

Ray: Is this denial of medical attention a form of torture, if not a
war crime? At the very least, isn't it completely contrary to
medical ethics? Don't doctors have an obligation to take care of
their patients?

Ratner: It's absolutely unethical for a doctor to withhold care. But
what may be happening here is that a prisoner goes to the clinic
and complains, but is never allowed to see a doctor; the intelligence unit is running the clinic, and the doctors are only seeing

people referred to them. But if any of the doctors know this is
going on and are continuing to participate in this, it's unethical.
It would constitute torture to withhold medical treatment from
somebody who was in great pain or needed medical treatment,
and it would most likely be a war crime.

Ray: We know from the Department of Defense's own statements
that one in five of the detainees are being medicated for clinical
depression. We know there has been a rash of suicide attempts.
I know you are not a medical expert, but I would like to know
what you think about the medical ethics involved here, about
the culpability of doctors observing and treating these detainees.

Ratner: I think it is unethical for doctors to be playing any role at
all in these interrogations. It is like a doctor watching someone
being tortured and advising the torturers how far they can go
without killing him, which would be criminal. Some of those
released say they were drugged at the whim of the com-
manders, and there are charges that prisoners who resisted the
injections were beaten. If the doctors participate in the coercive
techniques, it would be criminal as well as unethical. We have
learned, for example, that some doctors conspired in an
attempt to show that the suicide rate had declined, simply by
reclassifying suicide attempts as what they call SIB, "self-inju-
rious behavior," arguing that the individuals did not really
want to kill themselves. Reportedly, there were forty such incidents in the last six months of 2003.

Ray: One related question is whether a doctor should certify that
an accused person is competent to stand trial when the government wants that person to do so.

Ratner: The doctors who are opposed to involvement in such a
certification process point out that after you keep people in a
severely coercive environment for two and a half years without

them having any idea what they are charged with, you can't just
say, This guy understands the charges against him and he can
stand trial. By that time, the guy is essentially putty, somebody
the United States can do whatever they want with.

The staff psychiatrist at Guantánamo had the audacity to say
in an interview that he thought most of the prisoners suffering
from depression brought their symptoms with them. It is terrible having doctors play a part in this, if they are. It smacks of
what Nazi doctors did during World War II. It seems to me the
medical profession has an obligation to speak out, to say that no
doctor can ethically work with the people in Guantánamo. To
do so is to cooperate in an interrogation camp, a violation of
international law, of the Geneva Conventions.

Ray: During one court argument, the Bush administration took
the position that even if the plaintiffs were to claim their captors were engaging in the torture of Guantánamo prisoners,
U.S. courts would have absolutely no legal right to question the
administration's conduct.

Ratner: That is the amazing position they took. This all goes to the
question of whether Guantánamo is a lawless zone over which
no court in the world has jurisdiction, a place where the United
States can operate completely free of any judicial oversight.

This argument is, in my view, completely wrong, but it is why
the United States is putting people in Guantánamo. When we
represented the Haitian detainees who were in Guantánamo in
the early 1990s, the same assertion came forward. The court of
appeals asked the government's lawyers, does this mean you can
throw people overboard, you can torture them, drown them?
The government said, We would not do that, but in any case this
court would have nothing to say about it. This court cannot look
at what we do. We assert that the United States obeys international law, but this court cannot question whether we do.

Ray: In the case of Jose Padilla, one of the American enemy combatants, which was argued before the Supreme Court in April 2004, this question of torture came up again. Apparently Justice Ruth Bader Ginsburg was worried that unless the Court had the power to review government actions, torture could occur and the Court would be helpless to deal with it. She asked, "Is it just up to the good will of the executive, or is there any judicial check?" What response did the lawyer for the government give?

Ratner: He said, "Where the government is on a war footing, you have to trust the executive to make the kind of quintessential military judgments that are involved during war." Of course, he insisted that the government did not engage in torture. This exchange was particularly remarkable as it occurred only eight hours prior to the release of the Abu Ghraib torture photos on CBS.

Ray: The Bush administration says that all detainees are treated humanely "to the extent appropriate and consistent with military necessity."

Ratner: Right. That is probably the most unbelievably telling admission they have made. They are saying they will not treat people humanely if they think military necessity requires otherwise. In other words, they will treat the prisoners humanely, without torturing them, without stress and duress, without cruel and inhuman and degrading treatment, *unless* they feel they need information from them they cannot otherwise get. But in such case, they can and will treat them inhumanely. One official who supervised the capture of prisoners told *The Washington Post,* "If you don't violate someone's human rights some of the time, you probably aren't doing your job."

That is completely unacceptable, completely illegal. Every human being everywhere in the world has to be treated humanely all the time. It's hypocritical to torture a person when you think it's necessary and say that at other times torture is not ethical. You must always treat people humanely. It is a staggering admission of the illegality of the Bush administration's antiterrorism policies and a repudiation of the Convention Against Torture and of principles of international law that have been built up over hundreds of years.

Ray: There has been a lot of speculation that one deliberate goal of this incessant inhumane treatment has been the forced recruitment of detainees to become undercover agents for the U.S. government.

Ratner: This is a very important function of Guantánamo. This is exactly what the British did with IRA prisoners. Just as is being done in Guantánamo, they refused to give out the names of detainees for "security reasons" and kept them in detention for long periods of time. During that period, many of them were turned into undercover agents for British intelligence.

What is going on in Guantánamo is not just about interrogation, not just about keeping allegedly dangerous people off the battlefield, but about recruiting Muslim informants to go around the Islamic world, to go back to their countries of origin and get information back to the United States, essentially to spy for the United States. One possible reason that pictures of abuse were taken in Iraq was as a means to blackmail informants—to insure that they would do their jobs as informants, on pain of release of the embarrassing photos. Until we know otherwise, I think we need to assume that similar tactics were employed in Guantánamo.

Ray: I have seen reports of CIA, FBI, and British intelligence teams working side-by-side with the interrogators at Guantánamo, helping to decide who the likely recruits are and making the pitch. The prisoners at Guantánamo, held in isolation and beyond the reach of the law, must be a dream come true for them, part of the counterterrorist policy underlying the Bush doctrine of an endless, global war on terrorism.

Ratner: Whether this has anything to do with stopping terrorism is another question to me. The CIA stations around the world are not usually about stopping terrorism; they are usually about stopping democracy. They are more concerned with continued U.S. control in these regions than in actually making us any safer at home.

And there are some serious legal problems here. While the desire to have undercover agents and to get intelligence may be on the surface legitimate, it is not legitimate or lawful to recruit such agents by holding them in isolation for years, with no charges, under intense physical and mental deprivation, to turn them in desperation into your robots. It is obviously completely illegal.

The second problem is that these kinds of infiltration operations can backfire. Your agents can end up being your well-trained enemies. And the third problem is about undercutting the independence and national will of people, about insuring U.S. hegemony in those countries where these people are sent.

Rendition

Ray: Getting back to the use of torture, about a year ago *The Washington Post* quoted an official as saying, "We don't kick the shit out of these detainees, we send them to other countries so they can kick the shit out of them." What is this referring to?

Ratner: Well there are two interesting points to make. First of all, it is nonsense to say we don't kick the shit out of these people;

in fact the United States does kick the shit out of them. We can
cite a number of cases where that has happened.

I know of people in Guantánamo who were beaten. But even
more compelling is what happens at the U.S. detention facility at
Bagram Air Base in Afghanistan, where the United States admits
to employing extreme "stress and duress, " which in my view
constitutes torture. Of course, now we know about Abu Ghraib.
Now we knew that the United States itself employs torture. Such
denials are preposterous.

As for sending suspects to other countries, on a number of
occasions, probably in the hundreds, the United States has used
a practice called "rendition," or sometimes "extreme rendition."
This is when you deliver a suspect to another country, without
any legal proceedings or formal extradition, for interrogation.
You are rendering someone up to the authorities in another
country.

Ray: Aren't you then, in effect, outsourcing your interrogations
under torture?

Ratner: Yes. Say the United States has a person in custody they
want to interrogate, but perhaps he has a lawyer here or a rel-
ative making inquiries. The administration avoids any embarrassing situation by sending that person to another country to
be tortured and interrogated, and then simply insisting they
don't have him, that he is not in U.S. custody.

The Center for Constitutional Rights is representing the
victim of a recent case of rendition. A Syrian-born Canadian citizen and resident, Maher Arar, was on a plane from Switzerland,
returning to Canada from a vacation in Tunisia, on a flight that
was routed through Kennedy airport. The U.S. government, and
apparently the Canadians, suspected him of something, and the
United States apprehended him in New York and interrogated
him for a number of days and did not get what they apparently

wanted. So the United States delivered him up to Syrian security services for interrogation to get information out of him by means they couldn't use in the United States. And despite his Canadian citizenship, they then flew him to Syria, where he was born but had not been for more than twenty years—a country which, the U.S. State Department reports, consistently uses torture in its security services.

And there are other countries, allies of the United States, to which we have rendered suspects. Three of them are Egypt, Jordan, and Morocco; we render suspects consistently to these countries for purposes of torture. A CBS commentator recently estimated that there are hundreds of such cases around the world.

Ray: *The Washington Post* quoted a former CIA inspector general who claimed that the United States did not torture prisoners, but that if we got the results of others torturing, we could use it. Is that legal or not?

Ratner: No. First of all, to the extent the United States is implicated in either subcontracting or transporting people to another country for torture, the United States is equally guilty of the torture. Encouraging torture is also illegal conduct. The government cannot simply say, as Attorney General John Ashcroft had the audacity to say about Syria and Maher Arar, "Oh, they promised me they weren't going to torture this person," when the U.S. government knows that that country consistently uses torture, and sent him there for that very purpose.

Secondly, the general law is clear that for criminal trial purposes, you simply cannot use the fruits of torture. U.S. officials may say they are obtaining the information only for intelligence purposes, but that does not make it legal. By using it in any way, by asking for it in the first place, they are condoning the universally condemned practice of torture, and in my view that is also illegal.

Ray: What about other detention camps? What do we know about them?

Ratner: Guantánamo is not the only U.S. interrogation camp, but in some ways it has become the model for what the United States is doing around the world. Some prisoners are at various camps in Iraq such as Abu Ghraib, or in Afghanistan at a "high-value" detention camp outside Bagram. The stories of torture coming from these camps are truly disgusting. Some detainees may be sent to Diego Garcia, a base in the middle of the Indian Ocean that the United States leases from Great Britain about which we know virtually nothing. And we hear stories that the most dangerous prisoners are being kept on U.S. carriers and tortured there.

The United States is also running a major detention and interrogation camp in Bagram where similar reports of torture are legion. In fact, in December 2002, two prisoners at Bagram were apparently beaten to death while they were being interrogated. A *Washington Post* article about the incident never used the word "torture," but two army doctors acknowledged the deaths were from beatings, and they were ruled homicides. In May 2004, newspapers revealed that at camps in Afghanistan housing so-called high-value detainees, mock drowning—a type of water torture—was used to get information.

Ray: Let me ask you about the war in Iraq. No one knows how many Iraqi civilians are still being held in detention by the United States. Estimates ranged from 10,000 to 20,000 being held in prisons like the notorious Abu Ghraib, although many hundreds have been released since the scandal broke.

Ratner: We now know, after the horrifying photos revealed in the press, that U.S. troops at Abu Ghraib—apparently encouraged by military intelligence units, the CIA, and civilian interrogators—were using torture there, including sadistic sexual practices, to soften prisoners up for further interrogation. At least two prisoners died under this torture, and more than a dozen soldiers, including their commanding general, have been relieved of duty and are under investigation. In fact, the deputy director of U.S. military operations in Iraq admitted to CBS that this "was not an isolated series of incidents." As of May 2004 the United States said it was investigating some 37 deaths that occurred in its detention facilities.

Ray: Is there a significant connection between the interrogators at Abu Ghraib and those at Guantánamo?

Ratner: Yes. Before these abuses occurred, in the fall of 2003 a large team of military intelligence officers, under the supervision of Guantánamo commander Major General Geoffrey Miller, who had bragged about how many of his prisoners had been induced to "cooperate," was sent to Iraq from Guantánamo to demonstrate techniques designed to "get more information" from the prisoners. In May 2004, amazingly, General Miller was permanently transferred to Iraq as commander of all U.S. prisons there, including Abu Ghraib, to "help insure proper detention and interrogation practices in Iraq." The logical conclusion, of course, is that it was General Miller's orders that, at a minimum, opened the door to such abuses. Remember also that it was General Miller who brought the now dismissed prosecution against Captain James Yee, a Muslim chaplain at Guantánamo. Yee was charged first with espionage and then, when that didn't stick, with possessing pornography. In the end, that didn't stick either, and Yee was completely exonerated. That Miller would be appointed to head Abu Ghraib is real cynicism.

Ray: Despite the president's professed shock and his repeated protestations that "we don't torture people in America," isn't it true that the guards at Abu Ghraib were not doing anything

worse than what has been done in prisons in Texas, New
Orleans, New York, and elsewhere?

Ratner: It is obvious that the administration was shocked only
because the photos had been taken and leaked to the press, not
because of what had happened. In fact, the guards who have
now been charged had earlier been congratulated for their suc-
cess in "priming" the prisoners for interrogation and in "getting
positive results and information." *The New York Times* had an
excellent article pointing out that a number of the practices seen
in the photos, such as forcing prisoners to strip and wear
women's underwear, are not uncommon in certain U.S. prisons.

Ray: What effect does the administration's attitude toward torture
have on the people committing, allowing, condoning, or
averting their eyes from it?

Ratner: The legal memos to the president and from the Justice
Department regarding the Geneva Conventions and the War
Crimes Statute, which makes criminal serious violation of
the Geneva Conventions (particularly with regard to treatment of prisoners), demonstrate that, at least since the war in
Afghanistan, the administration was planning to treat prisoners inhumanely. Moreover, the memos indicate that the
administration feared criminal prosecution for doing so.

The condoning of outlawed methods of interrogation by
those at the top obviously affects the people who practice those
techniques. Bush's actions take us all back to the Inquisition; it
really is medieval. We have to be aware that allowing
Americans to engage in torture corrodes the moral fabric of
our society. To the extent that a civilized society remains in this
country, and to the extent that we have any remaining values,
they are seriously endangered.

CHAPTER THREE

GUANTÁNAMO: TESTIMONY AND CASE DETAILS

False Confessions

Ray: The Center for Constitutional Rights currently represents two Australians, David Hicks and Mamdouh Habib, and two young men from England, Shafiq Rasul and Asif Iqbal. I understand that those four were your clients in the Supreme Court case. What can you tell us about David Hicks, the first CCR detainee case?

Ratner: Hicks was picked up in Afghanistan, allegedly on the battlefield but by the Northern Alliance, not by Americans. In January 2002, Defense Secretary Rumsfeld claimed that Hicks, an alleged Australian Taliban fighter, was someone who had threatened to kill Americans, one of the "worst of the worst."

Soon after his capture in Afghanistan, Hicks was beaten extensively during at least one interrogation, and was shackled and denied sleep for long periods. He spent time on U.S. Navy warships, where interrogations apparently took place, and at the Bagram air base, north of Kabul, before being sent to Guantánamo. He has been detained there as an "unlawful combatant" for more than two years without charge.

Ray: Some of the people who were released, among them two of your clients, have either falsely confessed or, as the U.S. military has said, no longer have any intelligence value. What do you think this means?

Ratner: Remember that Rumsfeld called these people the worst of the worst, the hardest of the hard core, people who tried to kill tens of thousands of Americans. And yet we see that even according to their own internal documents, U.S. officials knew that wasn't the case. Rumsfeld was lying to the American people from the very beginning.

A lot of these prisoners confessed to various crimes and supposedly divulged various sorts of intelligence information. But in fact, after two and a half years of incarceration in cages, with no hope of release, people will say anything if it's going to get them a meal, if it's going to stop them from being interrogated, if it's going to get them a toothbrush. This is well known to anybody who studies confessions. At Guantánamo, one of the rewards for talking is a shower. Another is the opportunity to get some exercise. After two years and two hundred interrogations, any of the most minor creature comforts will get people to say almost anything.

Ray: Some of your clients provide examples of this, don't they?

Ratner: Yes. Some of our clients who were released were kept in Bagram and then Guantánamo for almost the entire two-year period. The United States showed them videotapes in which they were purportedly depicted with Osama bin Laden.

At first they maintained that it wasn't them in the videos, but eventually they confessed that it was. These confessions turned out to be utterly false and were obviously coerced by the United States. We know this because eventually British intelligence, under growing pressure in Britain to investigate the prisoners' claims of innocence, proved to the American government that the men were actually in the United Kingdom at the time the videotape was made.

Some of the released British detainees had been picked up by the troops of a Northern Alliance warlord working with the Americans, Rachid Dostom. They were some of the many thousands of people packed into steel shipping containers in which thousands died; thirty to fifty out of each container of three to four hundred survived. They then were taken to Sheberghan prison for more than a month of interrogation and treated awfully.

Then they were taken in chains, trussed like chickens with goggles over their heads so they couldn't see, to Kandahar, where they were subjected to very heavy interrogations: forced to kneel, beaten on their backs.

Ray: Some of the British citizens at Guantánamo were not released. Tell us about them.

Ratner: There were nine British subjects at Guantánamo, and only five have been released. One of those still being held, for example, is Moazzam Begg, the son of Azmat Begg, a banker from Birmingham, England. Moazzam Begg was one of six Guantánamo detainees designated for a possible military commission. As of now, he has not yet been charged.

His story shows the administration's utter disregard for people's rights. Begg went to Afghanistan with his three young children to be a teacher. Eventually, he wound up helping construct water wells in very poor communities. When the war broke out, he was living in Kabul; when the bombing started, he escaped over the border into Pakistan, where he rented a house. His father was in touch with him and used to talk to him there regularly.

And then one night American soldiers and Pakistani intelligence agents came to his house and in front of his children, grabbed him, stuck him in the trunk of a car, and took him away. He had a cell phone with him, and he called his father, who got a lawyer in Pakistan to file a writ of habeas corpus. The Pakistani government claimed they did not know where he was. Eventually, when the judge was about to hold the interior minister in contempt, it was revealed that he had been turned over to the Americans.

The Americans apparently took him back into Afghanistan, and he eventually arrived at the notorious Bagram interrogation center, a place where we believe torture is being practiced. Begg spent approximately a year in Bagram. We don't know much about what he did there. His father got one or two heavily censored letters, in one of which he said that he never saw the sun or the moon, that he hadn't seen daylight for at least nine months in Bagram. Because of the censorship, of course, we don't know if he was tortured or if he tried to write anything about torture.

After a year in Bagram, he was transferred to Guantánamo, where he remains today. There are rumors that he is in terrible shape, which is one reason his father, an eloquent advocate for fair hearings for the prisoners, has not heard from him since mid-2003.

Azmat Begg says, in substance, "Look, I don't know what my son did or didn't do, but the idea that he isn't getting any kind of trial is outrageous." The United States claims the prisoners are free to write letters, but Mr. Begg has not heard from his son in many months. He may have been tortured; he may be in no mental shape to write.

Guantánamo as a Model for Iraq

Ray: On May 13, 2004, two of CCR's British clients sent an open letter to President Bush and some members of Congress (see

Appendix One: Documents). In it, they stated that military officials regularly used humiliating and degrading techniques that led to false confessions. Among the techniques they describe are short-shackling, whereby detainees are forced to squat for hours with their hands chained between their legs and fastened to the floor; being left naked and chained to the floor while women are brought into the room, a particularly humiliating experience for prisoners from strict Islamic backgrounds; and assaults and beatings so severe that hospitalization was required. Can you comment on this testimony?

Ratner: What is amazing to me is that these allegations are consistent with much of what has been revealed about interrogation abuse in Iraq, demonstrating that what was first used in Guantánamo was then used in Iraq. The Red Cross was apparently quite critical of these Guantánamo techniques and has issued a nonpublic report. That report, which a reporter has described to me, confirms what the letter reveals: short-shackling, chaining to the floor, stripping, and stress-and-duress physical positions. This and reports from other former prisoners are pretty shocking, and they certainly confirm our clients' credibility.

Ray: The government in its brief to the Supreme Court in the Guantánamo cases claimed that the people in Guantánamo were treated humanely. Is that the case?

Ratner: The government, in its brief before the Supreme Court, asserted that the people in Guantánamo were given three meals a day, given medical care, allowed religious worship, given mail, and given Red Cross visits to check on their conditions. But when you go through those five aspects of treatment, as well as others, you can see, based upon what has been publicly revealed, that the detainees were not being treated humanely. The entire operation—everything, from what you eat to where you sleep to what level of prison you're in—is run by the intelligence people, whom the detainees refer to as Intel. Nobody, not the Red Cross, not even your own guards, really has any power to change anything. It's all about intelligence and breaking people down and making them talk.

For example, meals are withheld or changed or just plain bad, depending on whether or not they consider you to be cooperating. In one case, a person who was clearly allergic to fish was given fish three times a day. So meals are used not only as a reward, but as punishment.

Secondly, the United States brags that the prisoners are getting better medical care than they got in Afghanistan or in Pakistan; but the prisoners have said that medical care, like meals, is withheld if you don't cooperate. If you have some kind of pain or you need some sort of medicine, they won't give it to you unless you cooperate.

The government claims that the prisoners have freedom of religious worship. But copies of the Koran, the holy book of Islam, were frequently stepped on and smashed by prison guards.

The fourth aspect of treatment is mail. The United States claims in its briefs that prisoners can send and receive mail, although censored. But one of our clients has not received a letter for two years. Intelligence officers hold up their mail.

One detainee was told that the interrogators had letters from his family and that he would he get to see these letters only if he cooperated with them, if he talked to them. And so, even though there is theoretically an absolute right to get mail—through the Red Cross and under the Geneva Conventions—prison officials are using deprivation of mail as a hammer to try and get cooperation.

The fifth area is Red Cross visits. Again, the Red Cross is supposed to have access to any detainee it wants to see. However, when the Red Cross visited one of the detainees, they asked his name, and when he gave it to them they said, "Oh, you're on our list. We don't get to see you." What was really going on was the United States not letting the Red Cross see people they wanted to put more pressure on. The United States has now admitted that, with regard to Iraq, it not only hid certain prisoners from the Red Cross, but also requested that the Red Cross give notice of its visits. Like similar actions taken in Guantánamo, this was an effort to avoid detection of its illegal interrogation methods.

So not one of the five things the United States claims in its brief to be doing to ensure humane treatment is really being done.

They had other ways of punishing people and trying to make them cooperate. I was told of one detainee who spoke only English and was put next to Arabic-speaking prisoners, so that he was truly isolated as a way of putting more pressure on him or simply making his life uncomfortable.

Other kinds of misconduct included injections. Detainees have been pinned to the floor by the IRF Squad and given forcible injections. Detainees also said that after every meal they became groggy. They still don't know why; possibly just to keep them under control, under some kind of sedation.

Each person interrogated was also given a lie detector test. Whether you passed the test determined whether you got certain privileges, what level of prison you were at, whether you got a toothbrush, whether you got a cup to drink your water, what kind of meal you might receive.

The three questions asked in the lie detector test, and over and over during interrogation, were the same for everyone. One: Are you a member of al-Qaeda? Two: Were you trained at the Al Farook training camp? (This is a camp the United States claims was run by bin Laden in Afghanistan.) Three: Were you given any special weapons training while you were at that camp? They repeated those questions constantly.

Even If you passed the test, it did not mean your release from Guantánamo. And although lie detectors are quite unreliable, if you didn't pass the test you got your beard and your head shaved as a punishment, another attack on the Muslim religion of the detainees.

Other means of harassing people included guards spitting in food, which happened on occasion. Another method of getting people to talk was by using false stories. For example, prisoners were told, "Well, you better talk to us because we were in a cave in Afghanistan and we found Osama bin Laden's records, and your name was on a list, and you're one of the five most wanted people in the world right now." Of course they would never show the list, because no such list existed, and no such cave existed, and no such records existed.

In some cases, they also intimidated prisoners with family photos that had been sent to them. The guards enlarged the pictures and put them on the wall, threatening that things would happen to the prisoner's family unless the prisoner talked. This is also a form of torture; you are not allowed to threaten someone's family to make them talk.

I also heard of a rather strange interrogation technique that I didn't really understand. In one interrogation room there were posters of Palestinian women who had apparently been killed by the Israelis. They were told, "You see what's happening to your brothers and sisters in Palestine? They're getting murdered and killed. If you want to fight on their behalf, all you have to do is cooperate with us, and we will release you to go fight on behalf of the Palestinians." It just didn't make a lot of sense to me, but then the whole camp doesn't make a lot of sense to me.

Ray: Possibly the interrogators were trying to gauge sympathy for the Palestinian cause, if there were Israelis among them.

The British

Ray: Nine British prisoners were picked up in Afghanistan and detained in Guantánamo. Five of them were released into British custody in March 2004, and on return to the United Kingdom, they were released in less than twenty-four hours. One of the released British prisoners was Jamal Udeen. What was his story?

Ratner: These rapid releases once the prisoners arrived in the United Kingdom indicate to me that the British detainees were wrongly held, wrongly interrogated, and wrongly treated from the beginning. The British certainly would have charged them upon their return if they had been able to.

Jamal Udeen was thirty-seven years old, from Manchester, England, a father of three. He had gone to Pakistan in October 2001 on his way to Turkey, traveling through Afghanistan. He had a British passport, and the Taliban picked him up at the border, probably thinking he was a British spy. They threw him into a Taliban jail, and when the Taliban were routed, Northern Alliance soldiers came into his cell and took him to the Americans, even though he was obviously a prisoner of the Taliban. Eventually he was taken to Kandahar, and then to Guantánamo. Today, according to one reporter who interviewed him, he walks with a stoop; the shackles bound him so tightly that he is permanently disabled.

Ray: How did some of the British clients find out that they were going to be released?

Ratner: The Red Cross visited them and told them that they would be released. But then the U.S. intelligence guys came in and said, "Look, we want you to become our informants when you go back to England, and inform on the Muslim community, and if you do, we will give you a nice house, all sorts of

things. And also we'd like you to sign a confession, because if
you don't sign a confession, you're never getting out of here."
But they knew they didn't have to sign the confession, because
the Red Cross had already told them they were being released,
so they just refused to do so.

This indicates two things. One is that the United States is
using this camp not just for interrogation but to create a stream
of informants all over the world. The other is that the United
States wanted to justify these unjustified two-and-a-half-year
detentions by trying, to the very end, to get the detainees to sign
confessions. Of course, they also hoped they could get them to
become double agents, and, as a former CIA officer told *The
Washington Post*, they wanted them to carry misleading intelligence back.

Ray: What more can you say about the British role in Guantánamo?
Ratner: I should point out that some of these five are considering
lawsuits against the British government for its complicity, as
well as against the U.S. government. The primary responsibility for this international detention camp is America's, but
other intelligence agencies around the world are working with
the United States, both in this camp and in others.

We know from lawyers in England that British intelligence
worked with the United States in trying to gain intelligence
from the Guantánamo detainees. The British were supposed to
be sending diplomats over to help get their citizens released,
but in fact British intelligence was working to try to build cases
against these people. Their British defense lawyers are now
blaming the British government for collaborating with the
United States to keep these people in prison.

The problem is not simply the United States. The problem
is governments around the world, Great Britain and the
United States in particular but others as well, including China

using these detention facilities as an unlawful means of extracting information from people.

Ray: Doesn't this imply that people are guilty until proven innocent?

Ratner: Of course. They have punished innocent people for two years. With any kind of legal hearing, these people would never have been jailed. The government even made the ridiculous argument before the Supreme Court that the prisoners get to tell their side of the story, by being interrogated.

The Afghans and the Pakistanis

Ray: A number of Afghans have been released. What are some of their stories?

Ratner: The stories of the twenty-three Afghans who were released from Guantánamo in March 2004 are consistent with the charge that the United States was detaining the wrong people. One detainee, Haji Osman, a fifty-year-old businessman, spent eighteen months at Guantánamo, and he never learned why. He was released after two and a half years, along with an eighteen-year-old cousin of his, and the Americans simply told him that they were sorry. They even imprisoned an Al Jazeera cameraman from Sudan for two years, for no apparent reason.

The Afghan stories are compelling. Some of those released said after they arrived home that they had been abused and deprived of sleep for weeks at a time. One, a prisoner named Mohammed Khan, said, "They did everything to us, they tortured our bodies, they tortured our minds, they tortured our ideas and our religion."

Another prisoner, Muhammad Sidiq, a thirty-year-old

truck driver from Kunduz, said he had been beaten, first at Bagram and then at Guantánamo. "They covered our faces," he said, "and started beating us on our heads and giving us electric shock." For two or three weeks he was going crazy, and then the beatings stopped, although he was often kept in chains. He slept in a place that was nine feet long and seven feet wide, and he could not see other prisoners most of the time.

Another prisoner, Aziz Khan, a forty-five-year-old father of ten, said he was taken because he had some rifles at his house. He was sometimes in chains, sometimes put in a place like a cage for a bird, sometimes kept in a freight container. He said, "Americans are very cruel. They want to govern the world."

Ray: The United States also released a number of Pakistanis in March 2004. What do we know about them?

Ratner: A man named Abdul Raziq was one of eleven Pakistanis released from the Camp Delta prison in Guantánamo. He had a master's degree in agriculture and was arrested in Afghanistan while on a preaching mission. They shackled him, sent him to Kandahar and later to Guantánamo. Another Pakistani, Abdul Mullah, a taxi cab driver from a village in Afghanistan, had been picked up for no reason, and he was understandably bitter about his experience. Another twenty-four-year-old returnee, Shah Muhammad, says the experience left him mentally disturbed. He said he tried to commit suicide four times while he was in Guantánamo.

Ray: One of those released, a Spaniard, was sent to Spain for possible prosecution. What is his story?

Ratner: Twelve prisoners were recently sent from Guantánamo to their own countries for possible prosecution. One of them, Hamad Abderrahman Ahmed, was from Spain. Even though he was sent to a Spanish prison, even though he may be prosecuted by the Spanish, he said "he was happy to have escaped the hell."

In an interview on Spanish radio he said that soldiers in Guantánamo stepped on his head as he lay face down on the ground, stepped on him and tied him up with a thin string that made him bleed. He denounced terrorism and the killing of women and children and said he had nothing to do with al Qaeda.

Ray: What other stories do you know about people in the camps?

Ratner: Well, for example, one person who had been picked up in Pakistan had been taken to Egypt, where he received electroshock treatments, which are apparently quite common there for political prisoners. Some of my other clients have also had such treatments.

Another person who was released about a year after the camp started claimed he was somewhere between ninety and one hundred years old. He was apparently one of the most pathetic sights, old and frail and barely able to get around the camp. He was chained with shackles to a walker. He was incontinent. When he would walk around his cell, or when he was let out for a little exercise, he would just cry all the time.

Some of the people released spoke of others sent to Guantánamo from Bosnia, via some other country, where apparently they were tortured as well. My clients said that the majority of the prisoners had been picked up in Pakistan by Pakistani police, not Afghanistan, and most of them were people who had been turned over for bribes and favors from the Americans. Most of them, almost all of them, were not fighters. They didn't think anyone was actually a terrorist.

The Children

Ray: Let's talk about the children. The Pentagon released three children between the ages of thirteen and fifteen who had been detained in Afghanistan on suspicion of fighting there. They were eleven to thirteen when they were arrested. And the Red Cross has said there are more children in Guantánamo. The government tells us that the children were treated very delicately.

Ratner: First of all, keeping children in a detention camp like Guantánamo is completely illegal under international law. The United Nations Convention on the Rights of Children says you can't do that; you have to begin rehabilitation and send them home immediately. Even if you think they did something wrong, they are still children, and they are to be treated under a juvenile justice system, not kept in a prison camp.

It was only after some complaints got out that the children were moved away from the other prisoners and put into a separate camp, Camp Iguana. But the continued presence of children in any prison camp is really an indicator of the whole outrageous situation there. And the stories of these three children are pretty harrowing.

One of them, Mohammed Ismail Agha, now back in Afghanistan, was probably thirteen or less when he was picked up. He says he was arrested by Afghan militia soldiers and handed over to American troops in 2002 while he was looking for a job. He was in prison for fourteen months as a terrorist suspect, two months at Bagram and then a year in Guantánamo.

He says he was guilty of nothing but looking for a job, and he lost a large piece of his life. It was ten months after his disappearance before he could get a letter to his father, who had been looking for his son all that time. He said, "When I was first captured, I was thinking they would not imprison me for long because I was innocent." When they took him to Cuba, he thought he would be released quickly; yet more than a year went by. This is a pretty outrageous case, but it fits the pattern of how the United States is treating not just children but everybody in Guantánamo.

CHAPTER FOUR

MILITARY COMMISSIONS AND THE SUPREME COURT

The Commissions

Ray: You noted earlier that a presidential order authorized military commissions for the trial of noncitizens. Have these been used?

Ratner: It seems that few of these commissions will be employed. When the rules for commissions first came out three years ago, CCR and others thought they would be widely used. They were to be used for trials of alleged members of al Qaeda as well as alleged international terrorists. However, as of May, only two detainees have been charged and only four others designated for commissions.

Ray: What is the government's explanation for holding commissions rather than conducting criminal trials of suspected terrorists in its custody?

Ratner: The government has labeled the people in Guantánamo enemy combatants. They are using that designation to imply that these people had guns, were found on the battlefield, and are part of a nation-state at war with the United States. They claim they are therefore subject to military law, even though they refuse to apply the Geneva Conventions. But would you call Timothy McVeigh, for example, who blew up the federal building in Oklahoma, an enemy combatant? There is a nice military sound to it, a suggestion that military law applies. But in fact he was a criminal—a terrorist to be sure, but a criminal, not an enemy combatant.

What the United States has done by using the term enemy combatant is to claim such persons can be tried under military law. But military law should not have any application to alleged terrorism. Even if it did, it would still call for trial by court-martial, an established system of military justice, not by military commissions, which are really courts of conviction.

Ray: From what you are saying, you don't think military commissions can deliver fair trials.

Ratner: The commissions were set up by the president's Military Order No. 1, issued on November 13, 2001. This order allowed for detentions, but also set up a special justice system for detained noncitizens. The order outlined the basics, and the procedural details were set forth a bit later, in Military Commission Order No. 1 of March 21, 2002, and subsequent orders.

People were quite surprised by the initial order, that the president was using a military order to try alleged terrorists. Terrorism by nonstate actors (those acting on their own, not on behalf of a nation state) is not a violation of military law or the laws of war; rather, terrorism constitutes murder, attempted murder, conspiracy to commit murder, or the crime of terrorism. The September 11 attacks were not part of an attack by a nation-state on the United States and therefore should not be treated under the laws of war.

Even if you believe that there had been a military attack on the United States that justified treating people under military law, this order did not call for regular, competent, impartial commissions or tribunals, such as courts-martial, that are normally used to try violations of the laws of war. Rather, the

military commissions are special courts set up by the president
to try people for crimes against the laws of war. I do not believe
they are legal in light of the Geneva Conventions of 1949 and
the International Covenant on Civil and Political Rights. In the
last American war-crime trial in the 1970s, Lieutenant William
Calley was tried for the My Lai massacre not by a military commission, but by a regular court-martial.

Ray: President Bush has been accused of executive unilateralism
in establishing these commissions. Could you talk about how
they fit with checks and balances of the Constitution?

Ratner: Our court systems are set up by the legislative branch, not the
executive. When military commissions were last used, during the
Second World War, there was congressional authority to set them
up. In this case, there hasn't been any such action. These are executive courts, set up by the president to try people the president designates for trial. Congress has been kept in the dark about the
administration's plans for the Guantánamo prisoners, both those
in custody and those who might be brought there in the future.

Consider the three aspects of a prosecution. First, one body
of the government defines what the crimes are. Second,
another body of the government prosecutes the crimes. And a
third body of the government adjudicates the guilt and determines the punishment. In our system of checks and balances,
each of those steps is taken by a different branch of the government of the United States. The Congress defines crimes. The
executive branch prosecutes people for crimes that have been
defined by the Congress in courts that have been established by
the Congress and the Constitution. The judiciary adjudicates
guilt and dispenses punishment.

In this case, the executive has taken all these roles unto
itself. The president and the Pentagon have decided that they
will define the crimes, prosecute people, adjudicate guilt, and

dispense punishment. This is unchecked rule by the executive branch. It dispenses entirely with our system of checks and balances.

Moreover, a convicted person normally has the right to appeal to a higher court. Under these military commissions, the only appeal is to an administrative board (also set up by the executive branch) to the secretary of defense, and then to the president. Here, the president has taken all the functions that normally are distributed widely in our government and put them in his own hands. If that's not rule by fiat or dictatorship, I don't know what is.

Ray: So virtually any act anywhere that gives the president reason to believe an alien is involved with an international terrorist organization can trigger a commission. Is that right, and is that fair?

Ratner: Yes, any noncitizen alleged to be an international terrorist can be tried by military commissions according to this military order. The order allows the president simply to designate a person to be detained and then tried. That is unique in our system. Normally the district attorney investigates and presents evidence to a grand jury, and then there is a hearing before an impartial court, set up by the legislature, to determine whether there is enough evidence to bring a person to trial. Now, a person can be bound over to a commission merely because the president designates that person to be arrested, detained, and tried.

There is no check on the president's power of designation, so he can simply name any alien anywhere in the world, and have the military go pick up that person. This is not hypothetical; the president has already signed such orders. It is an unprecedented power, and it is very frightening that any single person in the world should have this ability.

Ray: Are there legal precedents for these commissions, and do they have rules?

Ratner: The government cites *Ex Parte Quirin,* of which we spoke earlier. Commissions were, in fact, used quite often during World War II. But those aren't really precedents for what the United States is doing here.

First of all, the World War II commissions were authorized by enabling legislation passed by the U.S. Congress. More to the point, since World War II, principles of international law, embodied in treaties to which the United States is a party, have prohibited ad hoc tribunals or special commissions like those used in that war. Both the Geneva Conventions, which regulate military law, and the International Convention on Civil and Political Rights say that people can only be tried by regularly constituted tribunals that give full and fair hearings and that are impartial.

By "regularly constituted tribunals" they mean commissions or tribunals that are already set up, not created after the fact for something that has just happened. Ad hoc commissions or tribunals are inherently unfair because they've been set up with special rules for the specific purpose of convicting particular people.

Remember, the defendants are designated by the president, turned over to the secretary of defense. They are then investigated by the administration. These judges can decide how much evidence is necessary to convict and what evidence is admissible.

This is not an impartial judiciary, as we have in other courts in the United States. This is not a professional judiciary, as we have in courts-martial. The chief executive designates people to be both judge and jury and determines the rules of evidence.

A person charged before a commission is given a military defense attorney, also appointed by the executive branch. The defendant has the theoretical right to a civilian lawyer, except it has to be at his own expense, and so it is rather unlikely that most of those charged are going to be able to hire civilian lawyers. And any civilian attorney would have to have a security clearance, which gives the government veto power over any civilian lawyer.

Another major, fundamental defect in the rules is that the commission may allow any kind of evidence, as long as it's what they call probative—as long as it has some value, whether or not it would be admissible in a normal criminal trial.

Ray: The former commander of Guantánamo, Major General Geoffrey Miller, has said that three-quarters of the prisoners have confessed to something. How does this relate to the commissions?

Ratner: I am sure that by the time the commissions begin, the government will have all kinds of alleged confessions that in a normal court would be thrown out as coerced, as involuntary, as resulting from torture. But these commissions have no rule about keeping out coerced confessions. It is up to the hand-picked judges to decide how much weight or importance to give that evidence. It is all admissible.

The government is also allowed to use hearsay evidence, such as someone testifying that he heard someone say something about someone else; or affidavits from people who can't be cross-examined. The right of confrontation, which is embedded in our Constitution, will be dispensed with.

In addition, these commissions can be held in complete secrecy—not just when classified information might be divulged, which is normal, but whenever the government decides it is "in the interest of national security" to close the proceedings.

Also, although unanimity is required to impose a death sentence, only a bare majority of the judges are needed to convict, even of a death-penalty offense. The fact that a prisoner can be convicted of a death-penalty crime without a unanimous jury is pretty outrageous. In our normal, constitutional system, juries must be unanimous. The administration is easing every single rule meant to protect the defendant.

Ray: What sort of crimes can be charged in the commissions?

Ratner: The Pentagon issued a twenty-page list of possible crimes, all claimed to be violations of the laws of war. None of these crimes have specific sentences attached to them. When a defendant goes before a commission, he doesn't know whether he might get one year or twenty years or even the death penalty, because no sentence is specified. The only way a prisoner knows he might get death is if he sees seven judges trying him; the rules specify that seven judges are needed to impose the death penalty.

The proceedings violate everything we've ever known about justice, about international law, and about military law. They're really an abomination.

Ray: What is the status of the commissions, and when do they begin?

Ratner: Things are moving, but quite slowly. The order setting up the military commissions was issued in November 2001, over two and a half years back, and there has not been one trial yet. Perhaps they will begin just before the election in November, as some sort of October Surprise.

Some military lawyers thought the government would never actually try anybody in front of such commissions. The rules have changed continuously as major objections have been raised from across the political spectrum. Originally the government claimed the right to wiretap all attorney-client calls. Apparently they might withdraw now from that.

Finally, in August 2003, the president designated six people for potential trial by the commissions. We knew of three of them; one was our client David Hicks, the Australian, and two were from the United Kingdom, Moazzam Begg and Feroz

Abassi. We also heard that there were going to be some people from Yemen and Sudan.

But after that designation it became quiet again. No one was charged until February 24, when two of the original six designees were charged. One was Ali Hamza Ahmed Sulayman al Bahlul, a Yemeni said to be an al Qaeda propagandist who had allegedly produced some videos for Osama bin Laden. They charged him with conspiracy to kill and with aiding and abetting in the killing of unarmed civilians by propagandizing for bin Laden. The other, Ibrahim Ahmed Mahmoud al Qosi of Sudan, was charged with conspiracy to commit war crimes. He is alleged to be an al Qaeda accountant as well as a bodyguard and weapons smuggler for Osama bin Laden. But the charges against both of them are not only very vague and broad but also are based primarily on conduct that occurred before 9/11.

What's wrong with these indictments is that crimes like these can only be committed in the context of an international armed conflict. But there is no international armed conflict here between two nation-states, only a conflict between some members of a group called al Qaeda on the one hand and the United States on the other.

I should point out that as soon as people were designated for these commissions, they were taken out of the regular Camp Delta and put into Camp Echo, a separate camp in which they're completely isolated and cannot communicate with any other person.

Ray: How do the military lawyers assigned to work on these cases view them?

Ratner: The military lawyers have been aggressive about denouncing these commissions. They consider this situation outside any kind of legal system that they had ever known, and they have spoken publicly about it. They work under Colonel

William Gunn. Normally a military trial lawyer reports up a chain of command through military legal officials in the Judge Advocate General's command; but in this case they report to Colonel Gunn, and he reports to the Pentagon, to the office of the secretary of defense, right to civilian counsel in the Pentagon. These are clearly political trials; every decision is based on politics, not on law—that is why decisions are made by civilian appointees in the Pentagon.

Some of the most dramatic statements have come from Major Michael Mori, who was appointed to defend David Hicks. Hicks was expected to be the first defendant to go before a commission. However, as of May 2004, he had still not been charged while two others have been. At a press conference in London, Major Mori complained that the system did not provide "even the appearance of a fair trial."

His overall criticism is that when you use an unfair system, all you do is risk convicting the innocent and providing somebody who is truly guilty with a valid complaint to attack his conviction. It doesn't help anyone.

And Mori is not the only military lawyer to have spoken up. Two other lawyers appointed to defend al Bahlul, Army Major Mark Bridges and Navy Lieutenant Commander Philip Sundel, have also been extremely critical of the system. Commander Sundel told a Reuters reporter he did not think his clients had a very good chance to get a fair trial. And Major Bridges pointed out that the standards applied in World War II, which the United States wanted applied here, simply aren't acceptable today.

The military lawyers also filed an amicus brief in the Supreme Court case in which they made the argument that this commission system is an unfair system for trying people. So they've taken fairly dramatic action.

Ray: Have the military lawyers seen any clients yet?

Ratner: Initially, the military lawyers were not allowed to visit their clients, but later some were allowed to visit particular clients. These clients—Hicks, al Bahlul, al Qosi, and the remaining English prisoners—don't appear to be major targets of the United States. It may be that some of these people have been coerced over a two-year period into giving some kind of statements, and these statements may be false. The government may have expected immediate guilty pleas, with some quick sentences as a way to get the commissions moving. But that was in August, and nearly a year later there still have not been any guilty pleas, so it obviously hasn't worked out quite the way the government expected.

Ray: How are these commissions viewed in the Muslim world?

Ratner: They are the same kind of proceedings that the United States has spent many years condemning when used by other countries. The United States condemned the use of such a commission or tribunal against Lori Berenson in Peru. They condemned the use of such a tribunal against Ken Saro-Wiwa in Nigeria. For many years the United States has had a strong position against the use of military commissions or military tribunals. Now, under Bush, instead of trying to limit these proceedings in other parts of the world, the United States is creating an example that other countries will follow.

How can all this look to the Muslim world? It is obviously in the interest of the United States to make our country less hated among the peoples of the world—Muslims and others—and the way to do that is not to set up an obviously unfair system of kangaroo courts that try only Muslims. We should have a fair and open system in which people can participate, in which people get a fair trial.

The Supreme Court and Guantánamo

Ray: On April 20, 2004, the Supreme Court heard arguments in the Guantánamo cases. What were the legal proceedings in the federal courts leading up to those arguments?

Ratner: The Center for Constitutional Rights began these cases by filing a writ of habeas corpus on behalf of three Guantánamo detainees in the lowest federal court, the District Court for the District of Columbia. We filed in February 2002, and the case took more than two years to get to the Supreme Court. We were joined by another law firm, Shearman & Sterling, which represented twelve Kuwaiti detainees. Both cases were considered together throughout the proceedings.

We lost the case in the district court. The judge bought the government's argument hook, line, and sinker and said the court had no jurisdiction to hear the case, that aliens held outside the United States have no right to habeas corpus and no constitutional rights whatsoever. Our clients could not even get into court; their claim could not even be heard.

We tried to argue that because Guantánamo Bay Naval Station is under the complete jurisdiction and control of the United States, it is akin to sovereign U.S. territory. If a member of the U.S. military commits a crime in Guantánamo, that crime is tried by the United States under U.S. law.

The government argued that no American court, nor any other court for that matter, had any jurisdiction over any cases coming out of Guantánamo. The government pinned its argument on the claims that the United States does not have "ultimate sovereignty" over Guantánamo, without ever defining what "sovereignty" means. This will undoubtedly be their argument in the future for holding detainees without court review on U.S. military bases in Iraq, Afghanistan, and elsewhere. These are the arguments that were laid out in the Justice Department memo to the Pentagon a few weeks prior to the first detainees being shipped to Guantánamo. (See Appendix One: Documents.)

We believe that a habeas corpus proceeding should be able to be brought in a U.S. court on behalf of anyone being held by the United States anywhere in the world, but Guantánamo in particular ought to be a clear case. The United States is the only legal authority there. The administration's position—that habeas corpus could only be brought by someone inside the United States—was, we thought, just ridiculous. Still, we knew from our experience representing Haitians detained at Guantánamo in 1991 that the United States was insistent that no court had jurisdiction over Guantánamo. The United States wanted Guantánamo to be a law-free zone. And that is what the District Court ruled.

Ray: You then appealed that decision; what was the result?

Ratner: We appealed the decision of the District Court to the Court of Appeals for the District of Columbia Circuit, and we lost on the same grounds. It was a devastating defeat, and some of us thought it was the end of the road. We couldn't get a court even to say it had the right to hear our arguments. Nevertheless, we asked the Supreme Court to review the case. We had no right to demand they take the case, only to request that they hear it. We figured they would never take the case for two reasons: one, we were still living in the time of the so-called war on terrorism, and in such times the Supreme Court doesn't like to review executive decisions. And, secondly, we had already lost in the two lower courts so there was no compelling political necessity for the Court to take the case.

Ray: By that time, the prisoners had been held for a year and a half, and as far as is known, little or nothing of value had come out of the interrogations; Osama bin Laden had not been captured; no vast stockpiles of weapons of mass destruction had been found. How did the passage of time affect the public's perception of the cases?

Ratner: We had tremendous support by the time we were preparing our petition for review in the Supreme Court. Editorial writers across the country were asking what was going on in Guantánamo, why were there no hearings, how long can you hold people without a hearing or charges, contrary to the Geneva Conventions, how long can a situation like this go on?

Even if you believed that the government needed to interrogate these people, a year and a half had gone by, and there was no indication that anything significant had been learned in Guantánamo. By this time any intelligence would be quite out of date. Critical stories were coming out about people's treatment there. Some prisoners had by now been freed, and it transpired that many of them had been picked up wrongly, based on bribes or something else, from small villages where there had been no fighting.

In addition to the changing perceptions about the value of the Guantánamo interrogations, there was also a shift among conservatives, who worried about this level of unchecked executive authority. The idea that the government could simply pluck people from anywhere in the world and hold them indefinitely began to worry conservatives.

So when we asked the Supreme Court to review the case, we had an extremely broad group of amicus (friends of the court) urging it to take the case. They included survivors of the World War II detention camps for Japanese-Americans; former prisoners of war; former military people, including a general; former diplomats; and many other people across the political spectrum. The case developed a certain legitimacy it did not have at the outset; people were getting nervous about this previously unheard-of executive overreaching.

And then, after we filed, all we could do was wait, though

with little hope. It was a complete shock to us when, in November 2003, the Supreme Court said they would review the case of the Guantánamo detainees. However, they limited their review to a very narrow but crucial question that goes to the heart of whether the United States is a society governed by the rule of law: "Whether United States courts lack jurisdiction to consider challenges to the legality of the detention of foreign nationals captured abroad in connection with hostilities and incarcerated at the Guantánamo Bay Naval Base, Cuba." The court is thus considering whether its doors should be closed to people detained by the United States at Guantánamo. If we win, and the Supreme Court says the doors are open, it would then send the case back to a lower court to determine just what rights people held at Guantánamo have.

If we lose, it would effectively mean that no Guantánamo detainee could ever test his detention. It would be a disaster for a country that claims to adhere to the rule of law. In effect, it would also mean that no noncitizen detained by the United States anywhere in the world outside of the fifty States could test the validity of his or her imprisonment in a court. Detention by the executive branch would be unchecked by any judicial review.

The administration saw this decision—even to review their position that no court had jurisdiction—as a slap in the face. High officials were really shocked by the notion that the Supreme Court could review, and perhaps prohibit, decisions that the president, the commander in chief of the war on terrorism, was making. They believe that the president can do whatever he wants in that war, and that no court in the world can tell him otherwise.

The fact is that a majority of this Court, a relatively conservative Supreme Court, may have been offended by the notion that the administration could decide what actions of the chief executive the judiciary can and cannot review. Indeed, this is the essence of what federal courts do—review the legality of executive and congressional actions. The Court may have been concerned about overreaching by the president, about the question of whether a metaphorical war on terrorism justifies the wholesale abrogation of constitutional rights everywhere.

Ray: What sort of maneuvers did the administration try after Supreme Court review was granted?

Ratner: It was obviously very nervous and wanted to show the Court that it could be trusted. Shortly after review was granted, it announced they would be releasing up to 140 detainees in the next few months. This would be the first mass release. Of course, another reason for these releases is that Guantánamo has become a symbol of American lawlessness around the world, and the leaders of many countries were getting pressure from citizens who are working to free their countrymen. So the administration was throwing them a bone, hoping to lessen international pressure and attempting to combat the hatred the United States has engendered, in part because of Guantánamo. The administration was obviously scrambling. It even gave David Hicks—one of our clients designated for a commission—a military lawyer.

Deputy Assistant Secretary of Defense for Detainee Operations Paul Butler said that each individual case had been assessed by an integrated team of interrogators and behavioral scientists and regional experts, that individual detainees' cases were assessed according to the threat they posed to national security interests of the United States and our allies (see Appendix One: Documents). A few weeks after the Supreme Court arguments the Department of Defense established these panels and issued regulations for their governance. They also proposed yearly in-house reviews of each case to see if anyone no longer "dangerous" could be released.

Ray: What can you say about these assessment panels?

Ratner: There are serious problems. The new policy would create a three-member board of military officers to conduct an annual review of each individual detained at Guantánamo and make a recommendation about the continued utility of detention. But the final decision as to detention is made not by the proposed review board but by the designated civilian official (DCO), who is appointed by the president and works for the Department of Defense. Detainees can be ordered kept in detention, despite the panel's recommendation, if the DCO's opinion is that the detainee "remains a threat to the United States," or "if there is *any other reason* that it is in the interest of the United States and its allies" for the detainee to remain in detention. In other words, any reason at all can justify the detentions, even if the review panel decides otherwise.

These panels are totally one-sided. Everyone is working for the Department of Defense, and the person being assessed has no lawyer or spokesperson or advocate of any kind to say that, for example, they are using material based on coerced statements from other prisoners. These reviews don't offer any real legal protection (see CCR press release, in Appendix One: Documents).

However, these new rules and the other machinations all suggest that the administration was scrambling so they could go into court when the case was argued, and point out that they were doing something. They were telling the court, "You don't have to take action in this case. We are going to process people. We are going to do something with these people." And this is exactly what they said in their briefs.

Had we not been granted review, the government would have done absolutely nothing. They would not have moved an inch on Guantánamo. It is only because of this review—and the outcry both in the United States and around the world—that there has been any movement at all.

Ray: The United States claimed in the Supreme Court that it does not have sovereignty over Guantánamo, but could a prisoner at Guantánamo bring a case in a Cuban court against the United States?

Ratner: Well, the lease says complete jurisdiction and control is in the hands of the United States, so it's unlikely that a person detained in Guantánamo could bring any kind of suit in Cuba or anywhere else. And yet, while the United States claims Cuban courts would have no authority over this, at the same time, if a person tries to bring it to a U.S. court, as we have, they claim that complete jurisdiction and control is not sufficient for there to be U.S. jurisdiction because ultimate sovereignty resides in Cuba.

Ray: The United States formulated this doctrine during the first Bush administration, when Haitian refugees were rounded up and imprisoned in Guantánamo. You were directly involved in the lawsuits challenging those actions. Could you tell us more about them?

Ratner: The major issue for the government in those cases was making sure that Guantánamo remained a law-free zone where the detained Haitians had absolutely no rights under international law or under the Constitution. They went out of their way to ensure that that was the case.

Ray: And at that time, the United States managed to keep the U.S. courts from reaching a definitive ruling on the question of court jurisdiction over Guantánamo. But they have not been able to keep the question out of court forever, have they? How could the cases currently in the Supreme Court finally resolve this issue?

Ratner: Well, the cases in the Supreme Court squarely raise the question of whether any American court has jurisdiction over detainees in Guantánamo. There is also a separate issue: can U.S. officials detain any noncitizen anywhere in the world, whether in Guantánamo or elsewhere, and be outside of the court system? If a person is picked up and detained at a U.S. military base in Abu Ghraib, or Diego Garcia, or Bagram, is that person outside the court system? They should not be.

But even if the answer to that is yes, Guantánamo is quite different, as the United States has complete jurisdiction and control over the base. As the U.S. Navy states on its Web site about Guantánamo, it exercises "the essential elements of sovereignty over Guantánamo" and is the "supreme authority" there.

So what the Supreme Court will resolve, finally and presumably definitively, at least for a period of years, is whether or not non-U.S. citizens detained at Guantánamo have the right to to challenge their detentions.

U.S. officials are very clear on why they chose Guantánamo, as opposed to some other place. In Pakistan or Afghanistan, for example, there would still be (at least in theory) courts of that country where a person could challenge a detention. People publicly detained on Diego Garcia could presumably go into a court in the United Kingdom—which owns the remote island—to challenge their detentions. If you know the name of a person held in Bagram, you can conceivably go into a court in Afghanistan and challenge the detention. But if you keep people in Guantánamo, under the U.S. theory there's no court in the world that can take those cases. That is why people are in Guantánamo.

Ray: By the time this book comes out, the court will have ruled on the jurisdiction issue in your case. I would like you to anticipate, first, the worst possible ruling the Supreme Court could give, and second, the ruling you would desire.

Ratner: The worst possible ruling the Supreme Court could give is that no U.S. court has jurisdiction to decide any case of a noncitizen held outside the United States, whether in Guantánamo or not. In other words, the Supreme Court could decide that an alien picked up and held by the United States in a detention facility outside the United States and who has never had a significant relationship to the United States has no right to come into an American court.

That's saying that the United States can pick up noncitizens anywhere in the world, bring them anywhere they want outside the United States—Guantánamo, Bagram, South America, Egypt, wherever—keep them there indefinitely, and these people can never go to an American court to complain about it.

The Court could issue a more limited ruling that would be good for the Guantánamo detainees. It could say that because they're in Guantánamo and Guantánamo is under the complete jurisdiction and control of the United States, the Court has jurisdiction over cases from Guantánamo.

At that point it might simply decline to rule regarding people kept outside of Guantánamo. A ruling as to detainees in those places would be unnecessary to a decision in this case. No detainees from outside Guantánamo are before the Court; those cases would be left for another day. The middle ground would be this second, limited holding.

However, the most positive decision, the third way, and the one I think comports with the Constitution and international law and justice, is that any person, noncitizen or citizen, held in detention by the United States anywhere in the world can bring a writ of habeas corpus in a U.S. court to test the legality of his or her detention.

Ray: Assuming you win the Guantánamo case in the Supreme Court, what happens next?

Ratner: Well, the case would most likely go back to the lower court, the district court, which would need to determine the lawfulness of the detentions. The lower court would determine what rights the detainees have and the type of hearing they are entitled to in order to test their detention. The government would argue that the Rumsfeld panels are adequate; we would argue they are not. This could all take a long time. I hope the attention brought to the plight of the detainees, the public outcry, the pressure from other countries, in combination with favorable court rulings, will speed up the processing and release of the detainees.

Ray: What about Jose Padilla and Yaser Esam Hamdi? What are the legal implications of those citizen-as-enemy-combatant cases, and what are the best- and worst-case scenarios?

Ratner: We should discuss them separately. Hamdi was a U.S. citizen supposedly picked up on a battlefield in Afghanistan and brought to Guantánamo, where they discovered he was a U.S. citizen. Then they put him in a Navy brig in South Carolina. Because Hamdi is both a U.S. citizen and physically in the United States, there is no question about jurisdiction; the U.S. courts are open to him. However, there is considerable question about what rights he has and the proper scope of review of his detention. They still haven't given him a lawyer to litigate his case. They've given him one to talk to, but not to litigate the particular facts in the case.

The real question is whether he can challenge the government affidavit that describes why he is considered an enemy combatant, that is, that states he was found on a battlefield in Afghanistan with a weapon. The government is saying that all he can do, all his lawyer can do, is argue that the affidavit does not allege enough to make him an enemy combatant, which is ridiculous. He should, as a U.S. citizen being held by the United States, be able to argue that the United States has no

right to designate anyone an enemy combatant or, on the basis
of such a designation, to prevent him from challenging the substance of his detention in court, to challenge the underlying
facts and to examine the witnesses against him.

So the worst ruling in Hamdi would be for the Supreme
Court simply to say, We agree with the Justice Department and
with the lower court that he is not allowed to litigate the factual
sufficiency of the affidavit and that the affidavit based on hearsay
that he was picked up in Afghanistan is sufficient to hold him
indefinitely in a military brig without access to a lawyer.

Padilla is, in my view, a harder case for the government than
Hamdi. Padilla was picked up getting off an airplane in the
United States wearing civilian clothes. The government
claimed he was a "dirty bomber." Like Hamdi, he is also being
held in a brig in South Carolina, and like Hamdi he has been
denied an attorney. The government has submitted an affidavit
saying he has some relationship to al Qaeda, and he hasn't been
able to challenge that affidavit in any meaningful way.

But in the Padilla case, the intermediate court, the Second
Circuit Court of Appeals, ruled in his favor. They said that he
had to be released within thirty days or tried by a regular criminal court, because in their view, if you're going to hold an
American citizen in the United States you need a special statute
allowing you to do so, and the Bush administration never got
that authority from Congress. So two of the three judges on
that court ordered his release.

The worst ruling in his case would be, first, that the government is right that he can't have an attorney and can't challenge
his affidavit; and second, that a special statute requiring
authorization from Congress to hold American citizens within
the United States is not applicable in his case because the use-
of-force resolution against al Qaeda passed by Congress after
9/11 is, in fact, such a statute.

So there are two ways to lose those cases and both are quite harmful. In both cases the government essentially denied the habeas corpus petitioners the right to challenge what the government says in an affidavit, denied them the right to an attorney, and claimed there is no need for specific statutory authorization to hold them. Obviously, if Hamdi and Padilla, as U.S. citizens, have no right to an attorney or to meaningfully challenge their detentions, the detainees in Guantánamo will not have such rights either. So the scope of the relief they are given will be relevant to what ultimately happens to the Guantánamo detainees.

The best result in both Hamdi and Padilla would be that they are entitled to attorneys as soon as they're detained, that those attorneys have a right to meet with their clients privately and to examine the facts in the case, that they have a right to submit evidence to the courts, and that the government cannot use hearsay affidavits to claim that they're somehow enemies. Those would be very, very important decisions. And finally, it would be extremely important if the Supreme Court said you simply cannot use military law in these situations of alleged terrorism, but must treat people under normal criminal procedures.

CONCLUSION

Ray: Do you have any final thoughts about Guantánamo and what we have been discussing?

Ratner: Guantánamo represents everything that is wrong with the U.S. war on terrorism. The Bush administration reacted to 9/11 with regressive and draconian measures worthy of a dictatorship, not a democracy. They imposed the very measures they condemned in other countries: indefinite and incommunicado detentions, refusal to justify these detentions in court, disappearances, military commissions, torture. It was a descent into barbarism. The practices at Guantánamo spread to Iraq and other U.S. detention centers around the world. The U.S. government has obviously lost any moral ability to challenge such actions when taken by other countries. It has endangered people all over the world, not only by its own conduct but giving its imprimatur to inhuman treatment, which will embolden other countries to do likewise.

It has taken a thousand years to secure human dignity and basic rights for all. The struggle to do so is marked by moments like the signing of the Magna Carta in 1215, the Habeas Corpus Act in 1679, the U.S. Constitution, the Declaration of the Rights of Man and Citizen, the Geneva Conventions, the

Universal Declaration of Human Rights, the International Covenant on Civil and Political Rights, and the Convention Against Torture. The United States has now treated these landmarks of human progress as naught. Of course, there has never been complete adherence to these documents, but rarely, if ever, has there been such open, notorious, and boastful violation of fundamental protections as at Guantánamo.

But this is not to say that I am pessimistic about the chance of returning to sanity, enlightenment, and the rule of law. For the last few years, we have been in a long dark tunnel with no fresh air and no light. The president and his cohorts, who have brought us to this state, are in trouble: trouble in Iraq and trouble in Guantánamo. That even the Supreme Court appears to think so is a cause for optimism. We are at the beginning of what will be a long struggle to repair the damage that the government has inflicted on us all.

DOCUMENTS

Lease of Coaling or Naval Stations Agreement Between the United States and Cuba (1903)

Signed by the President of Cuba, February 16, 1903.
Signed by the President of the United States, February 23, 1903.

UNITED STATES GOVERNMENT PRINTING OFFICE WASHINGTON: 1932

AGREEMENT Between the United States of America and the Republic of Cuba for the lease (subject to terms to be agreed upon by the two Governments) to the United States of lands in Cuba for coaling and naval stations.

The United States of America and the Republic of Cuba, being desirous to execute fully the provisions of Article VII of the Appendix to the Constitution of the Republic of Cuba promulgated on the 20th of May, 19092, which provide:

> "Article VII. To enable the United States to maintain the independence of Cuba, and to protect the people thereof, a well as for its own defense, the Cuban Government will sell or lease to the United States the lands necessary for coaling or naval stations, at certain specified points, to be agreed upon with the President of the United States."

Have reached an agreement to that end, as follows:

ARTICLE I

The Republic of Cuba hereby leases to the United States, for the time required for the purposes of coaling and naval stations, the following described areas of land and water situated in the Island of Cuba:

> 1st. In Guantanamo (see Hydrographic Office Chart 1857). From a point on the south coast, 4.37 nautical miles to the eastward of Windward Point Light House, a line running north (true) a distance of 4.25 nautical miles;
>
> From the northern extremity of this line, a line running west (true), a distance of 5.87 nautical miles;
>
> From the western extremity of this last line, a line running south-west (true), 3.31 nautical miles;
>
> From the southwestern extremity of this last line, a line running south (true), to the seacoast.
>
> This lease shall be subject to all the conditions named in Article II of this agreement.
>
> 2nd. In Northwestern Cuba (see Hydrographic Office Chart 2036). In Bahia Honda (see Hydrographic Office Chart 520b).

All that land included in the peninsula containing Cerro del Morillo and Punta del Carenero situated to the westward of a line running south (true) from the north coast at a distance of thirteen hundred yards east (true) from the crest of Cerro del Morrillo, and all the adjacent waters touching upon the coast line of the above described peninsula and including the estuary south of Punta del Carenero with the control of the headwaters as necessary for sanitary and other purposes.

And in addition all that piece of land and its adjacent waters on the western side of the entrance to Bahia Honda included between the shore line and a line running north and south (true) to low water marks through a point which is west (true) distant one nautical mile from Pta. Dey Cayan.

ARTICLE II

The grant of the foregoing Article shall include the right to use and occupy the waters adjacent to said areas of land and water, and to improve and deepen the entrances thereto and the anchorages therein, and generally to do any and all things necessary to fit the premises for use as coaling or naval stations only, and for no other purpose.

Vessels engaged in the Cuban trade shall have free passage through the waters included within this grant.

ARTICLE III

While on the one hand the United States recognizes the continuance of the ultimate sovereignty of the Republic of Cuba over the above described areas of land and water, on the other hand the Republic of Cuba consents that during the period of the occupation by the United States of said areas under the terms of this agreement the United States shall exercise complete jurisdiction and control over and within said areas with the right to acquire (under conditions to be hereafter agreed upon by the two Governments) for the public purposes of the United States any land or other property therein by purchase or by exercise of eminent domain with full compensation to the owners thereof.

Done in duplicate at Habana, and signed by the President of the Republic of Cuba, this the sixteenth day of February, 1903.

(SEAL) T. Estrada Palma Signed by the President of the United States the twenty-third of February 1903. (SEAL) Theodore Roosevelt.

TREATY SERIES No. 426

LEASE OF COALING OR NAVAL STATIONS AGREEMENT BETWEEN THE UNITED STATES OF AMERICA AND CUBA

Signed at Habana, July 2, 1903
Approved by the President of the United States, October 2, 1903
Ratified by the President of Cuba, August 17, 1903
Ratifications exchanged at Washington, October 6, 1903.

UNITED STATES GOVERNMENT PRINTING OFFICE WASHINGTON: 1932

The United States of America and the Republic of Cuba, being desirous to conclude the conditions of the lease of areas of land and waters for the establishment of naval or coaling stations in Guantanamo and Bahia Honda the Republic of Cuba made to the United States by the Agreement of February 16/23, 1903, in fulfillment of the provisions of Article Seven of the Constitutional Appendix of the Republic of Cuba, have appointed their Plenipotentiaries to that end.

The President of the United States of America, Herbert G. Squiers, Envoy Extraordinary and Minister Plenipotentiary in Havana,

And the President of the Republic of Cuba, Jose M. Garcia Montes, Secretary of Finance, and acting Secretary of State and Justice, who, after communicating to each other their respective full powers, found to be in due form, have agreed upon the following Articles:

Article I

The United States of America agrees and covenants to pay for the Republic of Cuba the annual sum of two thousand dollars, in gold coin of the United States, as long as the former shall occupy and use said areas of land by virtue of said Agreement.

All private lands and other real property within said areas shall be acquired forthwith by the Republic of Cuba.

The United States of America agrees to furnish to the Republic of Cuba the sums necessary for the purchase of said private lands and properties and such sums shall be accepted by the Republic of Cuba as advance payment on account of rental due by virtue of said Agreement.

Article II
The said areas shall be surveyed and their boundaries distinctly marked by permanent fences or enclosures.

The expenses of construction and maintenance of such fences or enclosures shall be borne by the United States.

Article III
The United States of America agrees that no person, partnership, or corporation shall be permitted to establish or maintain a commercial, industrial or other enterprise within said areas.

Article IV
Fugitives from justice charged with crimes or misdemeanors amenable to Cuban law, taking refuge within said areas, shall be delivered up by the United States authorities on demand by duly authorized Cuban authorities.

On the other hand, the Republic of Cuba agrees that fugitives from justice charged with crimes or misdemeanors amenable to United States law, committed with said areas, taking refuge in Cuban territory shall on demand, be delivered up to duly authorized United States authorities.

Article V
Materials of all kinds, merchandise, stores and munitions of war imported into said areas for exclusive use and consumption therein, shall not be subject to payment of customs duties nor any other fees or charges and the vessels which may carry same shall not be subject to payment of port, tonnage, anchorage or other fees, except in case said vessels shall be discharged without the limits of said areas; and said vessels shall not be discharged without the limits of said areas other-

wise than through a regular port of entry of the Republic of Cuba when both cargo and vessel shall be subject to all Cuban Customs laws and regulations and payment of corresponding duties and fees.

It is further agreed that such materials, merchandise, stores and munitions of war shall not be transported from said areas into Cuban territory.

Article VI

Except as provided in the preceding Article vessels entering into or departing from the Bays of Guantanamo and Bahia Honda within the limits of Cuban territory shall be subject exclusively to Cuban laws and authorities and orders emanating from the latter in all that respects port police, Customs or Health, and authorities of the United States shall place no obstacle in the way of entrance and departure of said vessels except in case of a state of war.

Article VII

This lease shall be ratified and the ratifications shall be exchanged in the City of Washington within seven months from this date.

In witness thereof, We, the respective Plenipotentiaries, have signed this lease and hereunto affixed our Seals.

Done at Havana, in duplicate in English and Spanish this second day of July nineteen hundred and three.

(seal) H. G. Squiers
(seal) Jose M. Garcia Montes
I, Theodore Roosevelt, President of the United States of America, having seen and considered the foregoing lease do hereby approve the same, by virtue of the authority conferred by the seventh of the provisions defining the relations which are to exist between the United Sates and Cuba, contained in the Act of Congress approved March 2, 1901. Entitled "an Act making appropriation for the support of the Army for the fiscal year ending June 30, 1902."
Washington, October 2, 1903.
Theodore Roosevelt

Platt Amendment (1903)

Whereas the Congress of the United States of America, by an Act approved March 2, 1901, provided as follows:

Provided further, That in fulfillment of the declaration contained in the joint resolution approved April twentieth, eighteen hundred and ninety-eight, entitled "For the recognition of the independence of the people of Cuba, demanding that the Government of Spain relinquish its authority and government in the island of Cuba, and withdraw its land and naval forces from Cuba and Cuban waters, and directing the President of the United States to use the land and naval forces of the United States to carry these resolutions into effect," the President is hereby authorized to "leave the government and control of the island of Cuba to its people" so soon as a government shall have been established in said island under a constitution which, either as a part thereof or in an ordinance appended thereto, shall define the future relations of the United States with Cuba, substantially as follows:

I. That the government of Cuba shall never enter into any treaty or other compact with any foreign power or powers which will impair or tend to impair the independence of Cuba, nor in any manner authorize or permit any foreign power or powers to obtain by colonization or for military or naval purposes or otherwise, lodgement in or control over any portion of said island.

II. That said government shall not assume or contract any public debt, to pay the interest upon which, and to make reasonable sinking fund provision for the ultimate discharge of which, the ordinary revenues of the island, after defraying the current expenses of government shall be inadequate.

III. That the government of Cuba consents that the United States may exercise the right to intervene for the preservation of Cuban independence, the maintenance of a government adequate for the protection of life, property, and individual liberty, and for discharging the obligations with respect to Cuba imposed by the treaty of Paris on the United States, now to be assumed and undertaken by the government of Cuba.

IV. That all Acts of the United States in Cuba during its military occupancy thereof are ratified and validated, and all lawful rights acquired thereunder shall be maintained and protected.

V. That the government of Cuba will execute, and as far as necessary extend, the plans already devised or other plans to be mutually agreed upon, for the sanitation of the cities of the island, to the end that a recurrence of epidemic and infectious diseases may be prevented, thereby assuring protection to the people and commerce of Cuba, as well as to the commerce of the southern ports of the United States and the people residing therein.

VI. That the Isle of Pines shall be omitted from the proposed constitutional boundaries of Cuba, the title thereto being left to future adjustment by treaty.

VII. That to enable the United States to maintain the independence of Cuba, and to protect the people thereof, as well as for its own defense, the government of Cuba will sell or lease to the United States lands necessary for coaling or naval stations at certain specified points to be agreed upon with the President of the United States.

VIII. That by way of further assurance the government of Cuba will embody the foregoing provisions in a permanent treaty with the United States.

Military Order of November 13, 2001
(Military Order No. 1)

**"Detention, Treatment, and Trial of Certain
Non-Citizens in the War Against Terrorism"**

By the authority vested in me as President and as Commander in Chief of the Armed Forces of the United States by the Constitution and the laws of the United States of America, including the Authorization for Use of Military Force Joint Resolution (Public Law 107-40, 115 Stat. 224) and sections 821 and 836 of title 10, United States Code, it is hereby ordered as follows:

Section 1. Findings.

(a) International terrorists, including members of al Qaida, have carried out attacks on United States diplomatic and military personnel and facilities abroad and on citizens and property within the United States on a scale that has created a state of armed conflict that requires the use of the United States Armed Forces.

(b) In light of grave acts of terrorism and threats of terrorism, including the terrorist attacks on September 11, 2001, on the headquarters of the United States Department of Defense in the national capital region, on the World Trade Center in New York, and on civilian aircraft such as in Pennsylvania, I proclaimed a national emergency on September 14, 2001 (Proc. 7463, Declaration of National Emergency by Reason of Certain Terrorist Attacks).

(c) Individuals acting alone and in concert involved in international terrorism possess both the capability and the intention to undertake further terrorist attacks against the United States that, if not detected and prevented, will cause mass deaths, mass injuries, and massive destruction of property, and may place at risk the continuity of the operations of the United States Government.

(d) The ability of the United States to protect the United States and its citizens, and to help its allies and other cooperating nations protect their nations and their citizens, from such further terrorist attacks depends in significant part upon using the United States Armed Forces to identify terrorists and those who support them, to disrupt their activities, and to eliminate their ability to conduct or support such attacks.

(e) To protect the United States and its citizens, and for the effective conduct of military operations and prevention of terrorist attacks, it is necessary for individuals subject to this order pursuant to section 2 hereof to be detained, and, when tried, to be tried for violations of the laws of war and other applicable laws by military tribunals.

(f) Given the danger to the safety of the United States and the nature of international terrorism, and to the extent provided by and under this order, I find consistent with section 836 of title 10, United States Code, that it is not practicable to apply in military commissions under this order the principles of law and the rules of evidence generally recognized in the trial of criminal cases in the United States district courts.

(g) Having fully considered the magnitude of the potential deaths, injuries, and property destruction that would result from potential acts of terrorism against the United States, and the probability that such acts will occur, I have determined that an extraordinary emergency exists for national defense purposes, that this emergency constitutes an urgent and compelling government interest, and that issuance of this order is necessary to meet the emergency.

Sec. 2. Definition and Policy.

(a) The term "individual subject to this order" shall mean any individual who is not a United States citizen with respect to whom I determine from time to time in writing that:

1) there is reason to believe that such individual, at the relevant times,

(i) is or was a member of the organization known as al Qaida;

(ii) has engaged in, aided or abetted, or conspired to commit, acts of international terrorism, or acts in preparation therefor, that have caused, threaten to cause, or have as their aim to cause, injury to or adverse effects on the United States, its citizens, national security, foreign policy, or economy; or

(iii) has knowingly harbored one or more individuals described in subparagraphs (i) or (ii) of subsection 2(a)(1) of this order; and

2) it is in the interest of the United States that such individual be subject to this order.

(b) It is the policy of the United States that the Secretary of Defense shall take all necessary measures to ensure that any individual subject to this order is detained in accordance with section 3, and, if the individual is to be tried, that such individual is tried only in accordance with section 4.

(c) It is further the policy of the United States that any individual subject to this order who is not already under the control of the Secretary of Defense but who is under the control of any other officer or agent of the United States or any State shall, upon delivery of a copy of such written determination to such officer or agent, forthwith be placed under the control of the Secretary of Defense.

Sec. 3. Detention Authority of the Secretary of Defense.

Any individual subject to this order shall be—

(a) detained at an appropriate location designated by the Secretary of Defense outside or within the United States;

(b) treated humanely, without any adverse distinction based on race, color, religion, gender, birth, wealth, or any similar criteria;

(c) afforded adequate food, drinking water, shelter, clothing, and medical treatment;

(d) allowed the free exercise of religion consistent with the requirements of such detention; and

(e) detained in accordance with such other conditions as the Secretary of Defense may prescribe.

Sec. 4. Authority of the Secretary of Defense Regarding Trials of Individuals Subject to this Order.

(a) Any individual subject to this order shall, when tried, be tried by military commission for any and all offenses triable by military commission that such individual is alleged to have committed, and may be punished in accordance with the penalties provided under applicable law, including life imprisonment or death.

(b) As a military function and in light of the findings in section 1, including subsection (f) thereof, the Secretary of Defense shall issue such orders and regulations, including orders for the appointment of one or more military commissions, as may be necessary to carry out subsection (a) of this section.

(c) Orders and regulations issued under subsection (b) of this section shall include, but not be limited to, rules for the conduct of the proceedings of military commissions, including pretrial, trial, and posttrial procedures, modes of proof, issuance of process, and qualifications of attorneys, which shall at a minimum provide for—

  (1) military commissions to sit at any time and any place, consistent with such guidance regarding time and place as the Secretary of Defense may provide;

  (2) a full and fair trial, with the military commission sitting as the triers of both fact and law;

  (3) admission of such evidence as would, in the opinion of the presiding officer of the military commission (or instead, if any other member of the commission so requests at the time the presiding officer renders that

opinion, the opinion of the commission rendered at that
time by a majority of the commission), have probative
value to a reasonable person;

(4) in a manner consistent with the protection of information classified or classifiable under Executive Order
12958 of April 17, 1995, as amended, or any successor
Executive Order, protected by statute or rule from unau-
thorized disclosure, or otherwise protected by law, (A)
the handling of, admission into evidence of, and access to
materials and information, and (B) the conduct, closure
of, and access to proceedings;

(5) conduct of the prosecution by one or more attorneys designated by the Secretary of Defense and conduct of the
defense by attorneys for the individual subject to this
order;

(6) conviction only upon the concurrence of two-thirds of
the members of the commission present at the time of the
vote, a majority being present;

(7) sentencing only upon the concurrence of two-thirds of
the members of the commission present at the time of
the vote, a majority being present; and

(8) submission of the record of the trial, including any conviction or sentence, for review and final decision by me
or by the Secretary of Defense if so designated by me for
that purpose.

Sec. 5. Obligation of Other Agencies to Assist the Secretary of Defense.

Departments, agencies, entities, and officers of the United States
shall, to the maximum extent permitted by law, provide to the
Secretary of Defense such assistance as he may request to implement
this order.

Sec. 6. Additional Authorities of the Secretary of Defense.

(a) As a military function and in light of the findings in section 1, the Secretary of Defense shall issue such orders and regulations as may be necessary to carry out any of the provisions of this order.

(b) The Secretary of Defense may perform any of his functions or duties, and may exercise any of the powers provided to him under this order (other than under section 4(c)(8) hereof) in accordance with section 113(d) of title 10, United States Code.

Sec. 7. Relationship to Other Law and Forums.

(a) Nothing in this order shall be construed to—

(1) authorize the disclosure of state secrets to any person not otherwise authorized to have access to them;

(2) limit the authority of the President as Commander in Chief of the Armed Forces or the power of the President to grant reprieves and pardons; or

(3) limit the lawful authority of the Secretary of Defense, any military commander, or any other officer or agent of the United States or of any State to detain or try any person who is not an individual subject to this order.

(b) With respect to any individual subject to this order—

(1) military tribunals shall have exclusive jurisdiction with respect to offenses by the individual; and

(2) the individual shall not be privileged to seek any remedy or maintain any proceeding, directly or indirectly, or to have any such remedy or proceeding sought on the individual's behalf, in (i) any court of the United States, or any State thereof, (ii) any court of any foreign nation, or (iii) any international tribunal.

(c) This order is not intended to and does not create any right, benefit, or privilege, substantive or procedural, enforceable at law or equity by any party, against the United States, its departments, agencies, or other entities, its officers or employees, or any other person.

(d) For purposes of this order, the term "State" includes any State, district, territory, or possession of the United States.

(e) I reserve the authority to direct the Secretary of Defense, at any time hereafter, to transfer to a governmental authority control of any individual subject to this order. Nothing in this order shall be construed to limit the authority of any such governmental authority to prosecute any individual for whom control is transferred.

Sec. 8. Publication.

This order shall be published in the Federal Register.

Geneva Convention Relative to the
Treatment of Prisoners of War (III) Article V

Article 5

The present Convention shall apply to the persons referred to in Article 4 from the time they fall into the power of the enemy and until their final release and repatriation.

Should any doubt arise as to whether persons, having committed a belligerent act and having fallen into the hands of the enemy, belong to any of the categories enumerated in Article 4, such persons shall enjoy the protection of the present Convention until such time as their status has been determined by a competent tribunal.

Article 130

Grave breaches to which the preceding Article relates shall be those involving any of the following acts, if committed against persons or property protected by the Convention: wilful killing, torture or inhuman treatment, including biological experiments, wilfully causing great suffering or serious injury to body or health, compelling a prisoner of war to serve in the forces of the hostile Power, or wilfully depriving a prisoner of war of the rights of fair and regular trial prescribed in this Convention.

Available at http://www.unhchr.ch/html/menu3/b/91.htm

Convention Against Torture and Other Cruel,
Inhuman or Degrading Treatment or Punishment
(Part I, Articles 1-16)

Excerpt: PART I

Article 1

1. For the purposes of this Convention, the term "torture" means any act by which severe pain or suffering, whether physical or mental, is intentionally inflicted on a person for such purposes as obtaining from him or a third person information or a confession, punishing him for an act he or a third person has committed or is suspected of having committed, or intimidating or coercing him or a third person, or for any reason based on discrimination of any kind, when such pain or suffering is inflicted by or at the instigation of or with the consent or acquiescence of a public official or other person acting in an official capacity. It does not include pain or suffering arising only from, inherent in or incidental to lawful sanctions.

2. This article is without prejudice to any international instrument or national legislation which does or may contain provisions of wider application.

Article 2

1. Each State Party shall take effective legislative, administrative, judicial or other measures to prevent acts of torture in any territory under its jurisdiction.

2. No exceptional circumstances whatsoever, whether a state of war or a threat of war, internal political instability or any other public emergency, may be invoked as a justification of torture.

3. An order from a superior officer or a public authority may not be invoked as a justification of torture.

Article 3
General comment on its implementation
1. No State Party shall expel, return ("refouler") or extradite a person to another State where there are substantial grounds for believing that he would be in danger of being subjected to torture.
2. For the purpose of determining whether there are such grounds, the competent authorities shall take into account all relevant considerations including, where applicable, the existence in the State concerned of a consistent pattern of gross, flagrant or mass violations of human rights.

Article 4
1. Each State Party shall ensure that all acts of torture are offences under its criminal law. The same shall apply to an attempt to commit torture and to an act by any person which constitutes complicity or participation in torture.
2. Each State Party shall make these offences punishable by appropriate penalties which take into account their grave nature.

Article 5
1. Each State Party shall take such measures as may be necessary to establish its jurisdiction over the offences referred to in article 4 in the following cases:
   (a) When the offences are committed in any territory under its jurisdiction or on board a ship or aircraft registered in that State;
   (b) When the alleged offender is a national of that State;
   (c) When the victim is a national of that State if that State considers it appropriate.
2. Each State Party shall likewise take such measures as may be necessary to establish its jurisdiction over such offences in cases where the alleged offender is present in any territory under its jurisdiction and it does not extradite him pursuant to article 8 to any of the States mentioned in paragraph I of this article.

3. This Convention does not exclude any criminal jurisdiction exercised in accordance with internal law.

Article 6

1. Upon being satisfied, after an examination of information available to it, that the circumstances so warrant, any State Party in whose territory a person alleged to have committed any offence referred to in article 4 is present shall take him into custody or take other legal measures to ensure his presence. The custody and other legal measures shall be as provided in the law of that State but may be continued only for such time as is necessary to enable any criminal or extradition proceedings to be instituted.
2. Such State shall immediately make a preliminary inquiry into the facts.
3. Any person in custody pursuant to paragraph I of this article shall be assisted in communicating immediately with the nearest appropriate representative of the State of which he is a national, or, if he is a stateless person, with the representative of the State where he usually resides.
4. When a State, pursuant to this article, has taken a person into custody, it shall immediately notify the States referred to in article 5, paragraph 1, of the fact that such person is in custody and of the circumstances which warrant his detention. The State which makes the preliminary inquiry contemplated in paragraph 2 of this article shall promptly report its findings to the said States and shall indicate whether it intends to exercise jurisdiction.

Article 7

1. The State Party in the territory under whose jurisdiction a person alleged to have committed any offence referred to in article 4 is found shall in the cases contemplated in article 5, if it does not extradite him, submit the case to its competent authorities for the purpose of prosecution.

2. These authorities shall take their decision in the same manner as in the case of any ordinary offence of a serious nature under the law of that State. In the cases referred to in article 5, paragraph 2, the standards of evidence required for prosecution and conviction shall in no way be less stringent than those which apply in the cases referred to in article 5, paragraph 1.

3. Any person regarding whom proceedings are brought in connection with any of the offences referred to in article 4 shall be guaranteed fair treatment at all stages of the proceedings.

Article 8

1. The offences referred to in article 4 shall be deemed to be included as extraditable offences in any extradition treaty existing between States Parties. States Parties undertake to include such offences as extraditable offences in every extradition treaty to be concluded between them.

2. If a State Party which makes extradition conditional on the existence of a treaty receives a request for extradition from another State Party with which it has no extradition treaty, it may consider this Convention as the legal basis for extradition in respect of such offences. Extradition shall be subject to the other conditions provided by the law of the requested State.

3. States Parties which do not make extradition conditional on the existence of a treaty shall recognize such offences as extraditable offences between themselves subject to the conditions provided by the law of the requested State.

4. Such offences shall be treated, for the purpose of extradition between States Parties, as if they had been committed not only in the place in which they occurred but also in the territories of the States required to establish their jurisdiction in accordance with article 5, paragraph 1.

Article 9

1. States Parties shall afford one another the greatest measure of assistance in connection with criminal proceedings brought in respect of any of the offences referred to in article 4, including the supply of all evidence at their disposal necessary for the proceedings.
2. States Parties shall carry out their obligations under paragraph I of this article in conformity with any treaties on mutual judicial assistance that may exist between them.

Article 10

1. Each State Party shall ensure that education and information regarding the prohibition against torture are fully included in the training of law enforcement personnel, civil or military, medical personnel, public officials and other persons who may be involved in the custody, interrogation or treatment of any individual subjected to any form of arrest, detention or imprisonment.
2. Each State Party shall include this prohibition in the rules or instructions issued in regard to the duties and functions of any such person.

Article 11

Each State Party shall keep under systematic review interrogation rules, instructions, methods and practices as well as arrangements for the custody and treatment of persons subjected to any form of arrest, detention or imprisonment in any territory under its jurisdiction, with a view to preventing any cases of torture.

Article 12

Each State Party shall ensure that its competent authorities proceed to a prompt and impartial investigation, wherever there is reasonable ground to believe that an act of torture has been committed in any territory under its jurisdiction.

Article 13

Each State Party shall ensure that any individual who alleges he has been subjected to torture in any territory under its jurisdiction has the right to complain to, and to have his case promptly and impartially examined by, its competent authorities. Steps shall be taken to ensure that the complainant and witnesses are protected against all ill-treatment or intimidation as a consequence of his complaint or any evidence given.

Article 14

1. Each State Party shall ensure in its legal system that the victim of an act of torture obtains redress and has an enforceable right to fair and adequate compensation, including the means for as full rehabilitation as possible. In the event of the death of the victim as a result of an act of torture, his dependants shall be entitled to compensation.
2. Nothing in this article shall affect any right of the victim or other persons to compensation which may exist under national law.

Article 15

Each State Party shall ensure that any statement which is established to have been made as a result of torture shall not be invoked as evidence in any proceedings, except against a person accused of torture as evidence that the statement was made.

Article 16

1. Each State Party shall undertake to prevent in any territory under its jurisdiction other acts of cruel, inhuman or degrading treatment or punishment which do not amount to torture as defined in article I, when such acts are committed by or at the instigation of or with the consent or acquiescence of a public official or other person acting in an official capacity. In particular, the obligations contained in articles 10, 11, 12 and 13 shall apply with the substitution for references to

torture of references to other forms of cruel, inhuman or degrading treatment or punishment.

2. The provisions of this Convention are without prejudice to the provisions of any other international instrument or national law which prohibits cruel, inhuman or degrading treatment or punishment or which relates to extradition or expulsion.

Available at http://www.unhchr.ch/html/menu3/b/h_cat39.htm

Memorandum from Alberto R. Gonzales to the President

Decision re: Application of the Geneva Conventions to the Conflict
with Al Qaeda and the Taliban January 25, 2002

DRAFT
1/25/2002, 3:30 p.m.
January 25, 2002
MEMORANDUM FOR THE PRESIDENT
FROM: ALBERTO R. GONZALES
SUBJECT: DECISION RE APPLICATION OF THE GENEVA
    CONVENTION ON PRISONERS OF WAR TO
    THE CONFLICT WITH AL QAEDA AND THE
    TALIBAN

Purpose

On January 18, I advised you that the Department of Justice had issued
a formal legal opinion concluding that the Geneva Convention III on
the Treatment of Prisoners of War (GPW) does not apply to the conflict with al Qaeda. I also advised you that DOJ's opinion concludes
that there are reasonable grounds for you to conclude that GPW does
not apply with respect to the conflict with the Taliban. I understand
that you decided that GPW does not apply and, accordingly, that al
Qaeda and Taliban detainees are not prisoners of war under the GPW.

 The Secretary of State has requested that you reconsider that decision. Specifically, he has asked that you conclude that GPW does
apply to both al Qaeda and the Taliban. I understand, however, that
he would agree that al Qaeda and Taliban fighters could be determined not to be prisoners of war (POWs) but only on a case-by-case
basis following individual hearings before a military board.

 This memorandum outlines the ramifications of your decision and
the Secretary's request for reconsideration.

Legal Background

As an initial matter, I note that you have the constitutional authority to make the determination you made on January 18 that the GPW does not apply to al Qaeda and the Taliban. (Of course, you could nevertheless, as a matter of policy, decide to apply the principles of GPW to the conflict with al Qaeda and the Taliban.) The Office of Legal Counsel of the Department of Justice has opined that, as a matter of international and domestic law, GPW does not apply to the conflict with al Qaeda. OLC has further opined that you have the authority to determine that GPW does not apply to the Taliban. As I discussed with you, the grounds for such a determination may include:

- A determination that Afghanistan was a failed state because the Taliban did not exercise full control over the territory and people, was not recognized by the international community, and was not capable of fulfilling its international obligations (e.g., was in widespread material breach of its international obligations).
- A determination that the Taliban and its forces were, in fact, not a government, but a militant, terrorist-like group.

OLC's interpretation of this legal issue is definitive. The Attorney General is charged by statute with interpreting the law for the Executive Branch. This interpretive authority extends to both domestic and international law. He has, in turn, delegated this role to OLC. Nevertheless, you should be aware that the Legal Adviser to the Secretary of State has expressed a different view.

Ramifications of Determination that GPW Does Not Apply

The consequences of a decision to adhere to what I understood to be your earlier determination that the CPW does not apply to the Taliban include the following:

Positive:
- Preserves flexibility
  - As you have said, the war against terrorism is a new kind of

war. It is not the traditional clash between nations adhering to the laws of war that formed the backdrop for GPW. The nature of the new war places a high premium on other factors, such as the ability to quickly obtain information from captured terrorists and their sponsors in order to avoid further atrocities against American civilians, and the need to try terrorists for war crimes such as wantonly killing civilians. In my judgment, this new paradigm renders obsolete Geneva's strict limitations on questioning of enemy prisoners and renders quaint some of its provisions requiring that captured enemy be afforded such things as commissary privileges, scrip (i.e., advances of monthly pay), athletic uniforms, and scientific instruments.

○ Although some of these provisions do not apply to detainees who are not POWs, a determination that GPW does not apply to al Qaeda and the Taliban eliminates any argument regarding the need for case-by-case determinations of POW status. It also holds open options for the future conflicts in which it may be more difficult to determine whether an enemy force as a whole meets the standard for POW status.

○ By concluding that GPW does not apply to al Qaeda and the Taliban, we avoid foreclosing options for the future, particularly against nonstate actors.

• Substantially reduces the threat of domestic criminal prosecution under the War Crimes Act (18 U.S.C. 2441).

○ That statute, enacted in 1996, prohibits the commission of a "war crime" by or against a U.S. person, including U.S. officials. "War crime" for these purposes is defined to include any grave breach of GPW or any violation of common Article 3 thereof (such as "outrages against personal dignity"). Some of these provisions apply (if the GPW applies) regardless of whether the individual being detained qualifies as a POW. Punishments for violations of Section 2441 include the death

penalty. A determination that the GPW is not applicable to
the Taliban would mean that Section 2441 would not apply to
actions taken with respect to the Taliban.

o Adhering to your determination that GPW does not apply
  would guard effectively against misconstruction or misappli-
  cation of Section 2441 for several reasons.

  • First, some of the language of the GPW is undefined (it
    prohibits, for example, "outrages upon personal dignity"
    and "inhuman treatment"), and it is difficult to predict with
    confidence what actions might be deemed to constitute vio-
    lations of the relevant provisions of GPW.

  • Second, it is difficult to predict the needs and circumstances
    that could arise in the course of the war on terrorism.

  • Third, it is difficult to predict the motives of prosecutors
    and independent counsels who may in the future decide to
    pursue unwarranted charges base on Section 2441. Your
    determination would create a reasonable basis in law that
    Section 2441 does not apply, which would provide a solid
    defense to any future prosecution.

Negative:

On the other hand, the following arguments would support reconsideration and reversal of your decision that the GPW does not apply
to either al Qaeda or the Taliban:

  • Since the Geneva Conventions were concluded in 1949, the
    United States has never denied their applicability to either U.S.
    or opposing forces engaged in armed conflict, despite several
    opportunities to do so. During the last Bush Administration, the
    United States stated that it "has a policy of applying the Geneva
    Conventions of 1949 whenever armed hostilities occur with reg-
    ular foreign armed forces, even if arguments could be made that
    the threshold standards for the applicability of the
    Conventions…are not met."

- The United States could not invoke the GPW if enemy forces threatened to mistreat or mistreated U.S. or coalition forces captured during operations in Afghanistan, or if they denied Red Cross access or other POW privileges.
- The War Crimes Act could not be used against the enemy, although other criminal statutes and the customary law of war would still be available.
- Our position would likely provoke widespread condemnation among our allies and in some domestic quarters, even if we make clear that we will comply with the core humanitarian principles of the treaty as a matter of policy.
- Concluding that the Geneva Convention does not apply may encourage other countries to look for technical "loopholes" in future conflicts to conclude that they are not bound by GPW either.
- Other countries may be less inclined to turn over terrorists or provide legal assistance to us if we do not recognize a legal obligation to comply with the GPW.
- A determination that GPW does not apply to al Qaeda and the Taliban could undermine U.S. military culture which emphasizes maintaining the highest standards of conduct in combat, and could introduce an element of uncertainty in the status of adversaries.

Responses to Arguments for Applying GPW to the al Qaeda and the Taliban
On balance, I believe that the arguments for reconsideration and reversal are unpersuasive.

- The argument that the U.S. has never determined that GPW did not apply is incorrect. In at least one case (Panama in 1989) the U.S. determined that GPW did not apply even though it determined for policy reasons to adhere to the convention. More importantly, as noted above, this is a new type of warfare—one not contemplated in 1949 when the GPW was framed—and requires a new approach in our actions towards captured terror- ists. Indeed, as the statement quoted from the administration of President George Bush makes clear, the U.S. will apply GPW "whenever hostilities occur with regular foreign armed forces." By its terms, therefore, the policy does not apply to a conflict with terrorists, or with irregular forces, like the Taliban, who are armed militants that oppressed and terrorized the people of Afghanistan.

- In response to the argument that we should decide to apply GPW to the Taliban in order to encourage other countries to treat captured U.S. military personnel in accordance with the GPW, it should be noted that your policy of providing humane treatment to enemy detainees gives us the credibility to insist on like treatment for our soldiers. Moreover, even if GPW is not applicable, we can still bring war crimes charges against anyone who mistreats U.S. personnel. Finally, I note that our adver- saries in several recent conflicts have not been deterred by GPW in their mistreatment of captured U.S. personnel, and terrorists will not follow GPW rules in any event.

- The statement that other nations would criticize the U.S. because we have determined that GPW does not apply is undoubtedly true. It is even possible that some nations would point to that determination as a basis for failing to cooperate with us on specific matters in the war against terrorism. On the other hand, some international and domestic criticism is already likely to flow from your previous decision not to treat the detainees as POWs. And we can facilitate cooperation with other nations by reassuring them that we fully support GPW where it applicable and by acknowledging that in this conflict the U.S. continues to respect other recognized standards.

- In the treatment of detainees, the U.S. will continue to be con- strained by (i) its commitment to treat the detainees humanely and, to the extent appropriate and consistent with military necessity, in a manner consistent with the principles of GPW, (ii) its applicable treaty obligations, (iii) minimum standards of treatment universally recognized by the nations of the world, and (iv) applicable military regulations regarding the treatment of detainees.

• Similarly, the argument based on military culture fails to recognize that our military remain bound to apply the principles of GPW because that is what you have directed them to do.

Available at http://www.why-war.com/files/

Memorandum from Colin L. Powell
to Alberto R. Gonzales (Counsel to the President) and
Assistant to the President for National Security Affairs
Condoleezza Rice January 26, 2002

MEMORANDUM

TO: Counsel to the President
     Assistant to the President for National Security Affairs

FROM: Colin L. Powell

SUBJECT: Draft Decision Memorandum for the President on the
         Applicability of the Geneva Convention to the Conflict
         in Afghanistan

I appreciate the opportunity to comment on the draft memorandum.
I am concerned that draft does not squarely present to the President
the options that are available to him. Nor does it identify the significant pros and cons of each option. I hope that the final memorandum
will make clear that the President's choice is between

> Option 1: Determine that the Geneva Convention on the
> treatment of Prisoners of War (GPW) does not apply to
> the conflict on "failed State" or some other grounds.
> Announce this position publicly. Treat all detainees con-
> sistent with the principles of the GPW;

and

> Option 2: Determine that the Geneva Convention does
> apply to the conflict in Afghanistan, but that members of
> al Qaeda as a group and the Taliban individually or as a
> group are not entitled to Prisoner of War status under the
> Convention. Announce this position publicly. Treat all
> detainees consistent with the principles of the GPW.

The final memorandum should first tell the President that both options have the following advantages—that is there is no difference between them in these respects:

- Both provide the same practical flexibility in how we treat detainees, including with respect to interrogation and length of the detention.
- Both provide flexibility to provide conditions of detention and trial that take into account constraints such as feasibility under the circumstances and necessary security requirements.
- Both allow us not to give the privileges and benefits of POW status to al Qaeda and Taliban.
- Neither option entails any significant risk of domestic prosecution against U.S. officials.

The memorandum should go on to identify the separate pros and cons of the two options as follows:

Option 1—Geneva Convention does not apply to the conflict
Pros:
- This is an across-the-board approach that on its face provides maximum flexibility, removing any question of case-by-case determination for individuals.

Cons:
- It will reverse over a century of U.S. policy and practice in supporting the Geneva conventions and undermine the protections of the law of war for our troops, both in this specific context and in general.
- It has a high cost in terms of negative international reaction, with immediate adverse consequences for our conduct of foreign policy.
- It will undermine public support among critical allies, making military cooperation more difficult to sustain.
- Europeans and others will likely have legal problems with

extradition or other forms of cooperation in law enforcement, including in bringing terrorists to justice.

- It may provoke some individual foreign prosecutors to investigate and prosecute our officials and troops.
- It will make us more vulnerable to domestic and international legal challenge and deprive us of important legal options:
- It undermines the President's Military Order by removing an important legal basis for trying the detainees before Military Commissions.
- We will be challenged in international fora (UN Commission on Human Rights; World Court; etc.).
- The Geneva Conventions are a more flexible and suitable legal framework than other laws that would arguably apply (customary international human rights, human rights conventions). The GPW permits long-term detention without criminal charges. Even after the President determines hostilities have ended, detention continues if criminal investigations or proceedings are in process. The GPW also provides clear authority for transfer of detainees to third countries.
- Determining GPW does not apply deprives us of a winning argument to oppose habeas corpus actions in U.S. courts.

Option 2—Geneva Convention applies to the conflict
Pros:

- By providing a more defensible legal framework, it preserves our flexibility under both domestic and international law.
- It provides the strongest legal foundation for what we actually intend to do.
- It present a positive international posture, preserves U.S. credibility and moral authority by taking the high ground, and puts us in a better position to demand and receive international support.
- It maintains POW status for U.S. forces, reinforces the importance of the Geneva Conventions, and generally supports the

U.S. objective of ensuring its forces are accorded protection under the Convention.

- It reduces the incentives for international criminal investigations directed against U.S. officials and troops.

Cons:

- If, for some reason, a case-by-case review is used for Taliban, some may be determined to be entitled to POW status. This would not, however, affect their treatment as a practical matter.
- I hope that you can restructure the memorandum along these lines, which it seems to me will give the President a much clearer understanding of the options available to him and their consequences. Quite aside from the need to identify options and their consequences more clearly, in its present form, the draft memorandum is inaccurate or incomplete in several respects. The most important factual errors are identified on the attachment.

Comments on the Memorandum of January 25, 2002

Purpose
(Second paragraph) The Secretary of State believes that al Qaeda terrorists as a group are not entitled to POW status and that Taliban fighters could be determined not to be POWs either as a group or on a case-by-case basis.

Legal Background
(First bullet) The Memorandum should note that any determination that Afghanistan is a failed state would be contrary to the official U.S. government position. The United States and the international community have consistently held Afghanistan to its treaty obligations and identified it as a party to the Geneva Conventions.

(Second paragraph) The Memorandum should note that the OLC interpretation does not preclude the President from reaching a different conclusion. It should also note that the OLC opinion is likely to be rejected by foreign governments and will not be respected in foreign courts or international tribunals which may assert jurisdiction over the subject matter. It should also note that OLC views are not definitive on the factual questions which are central to its legal conclusions.

Ramifications of Determination that GPW Does Not Apply

(Positive) The Memorandum identifies several positive consequences if the President determines the GPW does not apply. The Memorandum should note that those consequences would result equally if the President determines that the GPW does apply but that the detainees are not entitled to POW status.

(Negative. First bullet) The first sentence is correct as it stands. The second sentence is taken out of context and should be omitted. The U.S. position in Panama was that Common Article 3 of the Geneva Conventions did apply.

Response to Arguments for Applying GPW to the al Qaeda and the Taliban

(First bullet) The assertion in the first sentence is incorrect. The United States has never determined that the GPW did not apply to an armed conflict in which its forces have been engaged. With respect to the third sentence, while no one anticipated the precise situation that we face, the GPW was intended to cover all types of armed conflict and did not by its terms limit its application.

(Fourth bullet) The point is not clear. If we intend to conform our treatment of the detainees to universally recognized standards, we will be complying with the GPW.

Available at http://www.why-war.com/files/

News Transcript from the United States
Department of Defense

DoD News Briefing
Paul Butler, PDASD (SO/LIC)
Friday, February 13, 2004—2:33 p.m. EST
(Participating were Paul Butler, principal deputy assistant secretary of defense for special operations and low intensity conflict, and Army Maj. Gen. Geoffrey D. Miller, commander, Joint Task Force Guantanamo.)

Bryan Whitman [deputy assistant secretary of defense for public affairs (media operations)]: Good afternoon and thank you for joining us this afternoon.

As most of you know, the secretary of Defense is in Miami today and has just spoken to the Miami Chamber of Commerce. And he touched upon the importance and the progress that's being made in the global war on terror and discussed the importance of our detainee operations that are taking place at Guantanamo Bay.

And to provide some more information on that, because there has been some interest in it lately, we have two individuals: Paul Butler, who is the Principal Deputy to the Assistant Secretary of Defense for Special Operations and Low Intensity Conflict; and Major General Geoffrey Miller, who is the Commanding General for Joint Task Force Guantanamo. And they're here today to talk to you about the importance of the Guantanamo facility and bring you up to date on some of our processes at that facility.

So with that, I'll turn it over to these two.

Butler: Good afternoon.

As the secretary indicated earlier today in his speech, the key insight I think into our policy at Guantanamo is that we remain in an active war with al Qaeda, the Taliban and its affiliated terrorist organizations.

And I think it helps just to remind ourselves on how we got here a little bit.

And that is that in 1996, Osama bin Laden issued a public fatwa declaring war on the United States. In February 1998 he issued another public fatwa and said—in which he said that it was the absolute obligation of his followers to kill Americans, civilian or military, wherever they could be found. After that followed the attempted millennium plot in 1999. Before that al Qaeda attacked our embassies in East Africa and killed over 200 people and injured close to 5,000. In October 2000, al Qaeda attacked the USS Cole, a warship in Aden, where they killed 17 service members and injured 39 others. Al Qaeda then made a recruiting video which celebrated that attack and was used as a recruitment tool for al Qaeda operatives.

And then, of course, there was 9/11, where close to 3,000 people died in one day on American soil; something that hadn't happened since Pearl Harbor in World War II; something that hadn't happened on the continental United States since the battle of Antietam; and an act that destroyed a building at the center of American power, which hadn't taken place since the War of 1812. Of course, the president responded pursuant to his duties as commander in chief. Congress endorsed the use of force in self-defense against those responsible for September 11th, and NATO and the U.N. Security Council both recognized 9/11 as an attack upon the United States.

In November of 2001, President Bush stated that, quote, "International terrorists have carried out attacks on the United States on a scale that has created a state of armed conflict that requires the use of United States armed forces." Close quote.

But unfortunately, that wasn't the end of the story. The war goes on. On December 22nd, 2001, there was an attempted bombing of a commercial transatlantic flight by shoe-bomber Richard Reid linked to al Qaeda.

In April 2002, there was an al Qaeda firebombing of a synagogue in Djerba Tunisia, which killed 19 people and injured 22. In June 2002, al Qaeda was likely responsible for a bomb that exploded outside the U.S. consulate in Karachi, Pakistan, killing 11 persons and injuring 51 others. In October 2002, there was a recording attributed to Ayman al-Zawahiri, bin Laden's deputy, saying, "God willing, we will continue targeting the keys of the American economy." On October 6, 2002, al Qaeda directed a suicide attack on the French oil tanker MV Limburg off the coast of Yemen that killed one and injured four. On October 8, 2002, al Qaeda gunmen attacked U.S. soldiers on Failaka Island in Kuwait, killing one Marine and wounding another. On October 12, 2002, al Qaeda affiliate Jemaah Islamiyah bombed the nightclub in Bali, Indonesia, which killed more than 200 international tourists and injured about 300. On November 28th, 2002, in Mombasa, Kenya, a vehicle containing three suicide bombers drove into the front of the Paradise Hotel, killing 15 persons and wounding 40 others. Al Qaeda claimed responsibility. That same day, two anti-aircraft missiles were launched, but missed downing a Boeing 757 taking off from Mombasa on route to Israel. Al Qaeda claimed responsibility for that as well.

On May 12th in 2003, in Saudi Arabia, al Qaeda suicide bombers attacked three residential compounds for foreign workers, killing 34, including 10 U.S. citizens. On August 5th, 2003, a car bomb exploded outside the J.W. Marriott Hotel in Jakarta, Indonesia, killing 10 and wounding 150. Once again, al Qaeda-affiliated group Jemaah Islamiyah was responsible.

Between February and October of 2003, bin Laden issued further tapes urging his followers to take up jihad and stating, "We stress the importance of the martyrdom operations against the enemy, operations that inflicted harm on the United States."

Between September 2003 and December 2003, Taliban militants stepped up the insurgency in southern and eastern provinces in Afghanistan, including attacks on innocent civilians and coalition forces. On November 15th, 2003, two suicide truck bombs exploded outside the Neve Shalom and Beth Israel Synagogues in Istanbul, killing 25 and wounding 300 more. An al Qaeda-related group claimed responsibility. On November 20th, 2003, two suicide truck bombs exploded near the British consulate and the HSBC Bank in Istanbul, killing 25, including the British consul general, and injuring more than 309. Al Qaeda claimed responsibility. In November 2003, Taliban bombings killed U.S. and Romanian soldiers and several Afghan civilians. In November 2003, al Qaeda also struck again in Riyadh, Saudi Arabia, killing 17 and injuring more than 100. In January 2004, Taliban bombings in Afghanistan killed soldiers from the United Kingdom and Canada. And since August of 2003, 11 U.S. soldiers have died in the war in Afghanistan.

This is not even a full, comprehensive listing of all the attacks but surely indicates that we remain at war with Osama bin Laden and al Qaeda. So when you put it in that context, what we're doing at Guantanamo Bay is not that surprising. We are holding enemy combatants in a global war on terrorism for security reasons, to prevent them from returning to the battlefield and injuring American soldiers and civilians—and civilians throughout the world.

So the law of armed conflict governs what we're doing here. Some people ask us, well, what about the Geneva Convention? And we believe that we—our policies are treating the detainees entirely consistent with the framework of the Geneva Convention. The Geneva Convention requires that combatants in a war fight according to certain rules, and there are several reasons why the enemy combatants at Guantanamo are not entitled to the full range of protection under the Geneva Conventions.

First of all, neither al Qaeda nor the Taliban were state parties to the Geneva Conventions. Second of all, they did not fight in uniform or subject to a clear chain of command. But most importantly, the Geneva Conventions were designed in large part to protect civilian populations, and al Qaeda, the Taliban and its affiliates, as you can see by that litany of events, deliberately violates those rules. Not only do they attack civilian populations, but they blend in with civilian populations, thereby increasing the possibility of civilian casualties. If the Geneva Conventions are to be enforceable law, there need to be incentives built in. And what kind of incentives would we send if we allow the full treatment under the Geneva Conventions to be extended to enemy combatants who deliberately and purposely violate them?

However, we are treating the detainees at Guantanamo Bay humanely and consistent with the conditions under customary international law for humane treatment. The detainees are getting three meals a day that meet cultural dietary requirements, they have adequate shelter and clothing, the opportunity to worship, including copies of the Koran and prayer beads, the means to send and receive mail, reading materials, and excellent medical care.

There is also a thorough process to determine who comes to Guantanamo. The secretary described this in his speech a little bit, but I'd like to give a little bit more detail.

First of all, there is an elaborate screening process that takes place in the field in Afghanistan. Over 10,000 detainees were taken into some form of custody; less than 800 have been brought to Guantanamo Bay. First, in a hostile environment, soldiers detain those who are posing a threat to U.S. and coalition forces based on available information or direct combat.

After an initial period of detention, the individual is sent to a centralized holding area. At that time, a military screening team at the central holding area reviews all available information, including interviews with the detainees.

With assistance from other U.S. government officials on the ground, including military lawyers, intelligence officers and federal law enforcement officials, and considering all relevant information, including the facts from capture and detention, the threat posed by the individual and the intelligence and law enforcement value of the individual, the military screening team assesses whether the detainee should continue to be detained and whether transfer to Guantanamo is warranted.

A general officer designated by the commander of Central Command then makes a third assessment of those enemy combatants who are recommended for transfer to Guantanamo Bay. The general officer reviews recommendations from the central holding area screening teams and determines whether enemy combatants should be transferred to Guantanamo. In determining whether a detainee should be transferred, the combatant commander considers the threat posed by the detainee, his seniority within hostile forces, possible intelligence that may be gained from the detainee through questioning, and any other relevant factors.

Once that determination is made, Department of Defense officials in Washington also review the proposed detainee for transfer to Guantanamo. An internal Department of Defense review panel, including legal advisors and individuals from policy and the Joint Staff, assess the information and ask questions about whether the detainee should be sent. There is also—that's part of the process.

Now, what happens once the detainee arrives at Guantanamo? Once the detainee is at Guantanamo, there is a very detailed and elaborate process for gauging the threat posed by each detainee to determine whether, notwithstanding his status as an enemy combatant, he can be released or transferred to the custody of a foreign government consistent with our security interests.

Each individual case is reviewed by an integrated team of interrogators, analysts, behavioral scientists and regional experts. Individual detainee cases are assessed according to the threat posed to the national security interests of the United States and our allies. Threat assessments are based on all available information from interagency sources and are provided to Southern Command for review.

During questioning of the detainees, new information is constantly revealed, confirmed and analyzed to determine its reliability. Unfortunately, many detainees are deceptive and prefer to conceal their identities and actions.

Some of you may be familiar with a document called the Manchester Manual. This was a document that was picked up in a search in Manchester, England and has surfaced in various other venues, including in Afghanistan. It's really the al Qaeda manual, and in it is a large section which teaches al Qaeda operatives counterinterrogation techniques: how to lie, how to minimize your role.

The commander of Southern Command or his designee then makes a recommendation in each individual case based on the threat the detainee poses to the United States as well as intelligence value or law enforcement interest. Those recommendations are then sent up to the Pentagon, where a group—a panel of experts from the Pentagon—from Policy, from Joint Staff, from the Office of General Counsel—collect that information and make a recommendation on whether the detainee should be released, transferred to the custody of a foreign government or continue to be detained.

Those recommendations are then sent out to an interagency experts group, composed of—not only of the Department of Defense, but the Department of Justice, including the FBI; the CIA; the Department of State; the Department of Homeland Security; and NSC staff. Each one of the interagency experts votes on the recommendation and the entire package is then sent up to the Secretary of Defense or his designee for review. A decision is then made on whether somebody will be released, transferred or remain in detention.

There are two components down in Guantanamo that actually

do this work. There is General Miller, the commander of JTF-GTMO, and his military intelligence teams that are debriefing the detainees for intelligence purposes. There is also a separate team called the Criminal Investigative Task Force, which is made up of components of Army CID, Air Force OSI, Navy NCIS, FBI and other law enforcement agencies, who also evaluate each detainee for threat and whether there is law enforcement interest.

I'd like to talk a little bit now about the process for transferring detainees. As you know, there have been over 80 detainees who have been released. There have been now five who have been transferred, including four to Saudi Arabia and recently one to Spain. Various factors must be considered before any decision to transfer to a foreign government is reached, including the threat posed by the detainee, any law enforcement interest in him or intelligence interest in him, and whether we can reach appropriate transfer agreements with the foreign government. This is a complex process, and we're actively involved in negotiations with many different countries about transferring their detainees to their custody. But we want—we're asking foreign governments to take responsibility for these detainees, to provide us with assurances that we think will address the risks that these detainees pose once they're transferred to the custody of the foreign government.

And that's because there are very dangerous people at Guantanamo. Enemy combatants at Guantanamo include not only rank-and-file jihadists who took up arms against the United States, but also senior al Qaeda operatives and leaders and Taliban leaders.

For example, enemy combatants captured during the course of hostilities include terrorists linked to most major al Qaeda attacks, including the East Africa embassy bombings and the USS Cole attack; terrorists who taught or received training on arms and explosives, surveillance and interrogation resistance techniques at al Qaeda camps in Afghanistan and elsewhere; terrorists who continue to express their commitment to kill Americans and conduct suicide attacks if released; terrorists who have sworn personal allegiance to Osama bin Laden; terrorists linked to several al Qaeda operational plans, including possible targeting of specific facilities in the United States.

For example, we have an individual in Guantanamo with links to a financier of the 9/11 plot, who attempted to enter the United States through Orlando, Florida, in August 2001. Phone records suggest that 9/11 hijacker Mohamed Atta was also at the Orlando airport that day. This individual was later captured in Pakistan after fleeing Tora Bora.

There are two individuals associated with senior al Qaeda members who were working on remotely detonated explosive devices for use against U.S. forces in Afghanistan.

There's a member of an al Qaeda-supported terrorist cell in Afghanistan that targeted civilians, especially journalists and foreign aid workers, and who is responsible for a grenade attack on a foreign journalist's automobile.

There's an al Qaeda member who was plotting to attack oil tankers in the Persian Gulf using explosive-laden fishing boats.

There's an individual who fought with an al Qaeda-supported terrorist cell in Afghanistan, personally establishing reconnaissance and ambush positions around the Kandahar air base.

There's an individual who served as a bodyguard for Osama bin Laden and escorted him to Tora Bora, Afghanistan, following the fall of Jalalabad.

There's an al Qaeda member who served as explosives trainer for al Qaeda and designed a prototype shoe bomb for destroying airplanes and a magnetic mine for attacking ships.

There's an individual who trained al Qaeda associates in the use of explosives and worked on a plot to use cell phones to detonate bombs.

And there's an individual who served as an al Qaeda translator and managed operating funds for al Qaeda and who helped stock-pile weapons for use against U.S. forces in Afghanistan.

These examples are merely illustrative, they're not comprehensive. But they demonstrate the importance in maintaining the security of the United States by holding dangerous enemy combatants off the battlefield.

Now, the intelligence—I would like to talk a little bit about the intelligence that we're gaining from these individuals because that's a substantial part of the mission at Guantanamo. And perhaps General Miller could address that a little bit later. But these individuals are providing us important information, which General Miller likes to refer to as "the golden threads of intelligence" that help us understand the al Qaeda network and to help us defend ourselves against them.

Now, I mentioned there are three basic ways in which the enemy combatants are categorized down there: those who will potentially be eligible for release, those who will be eligible for transfer to their foreign governments, and those who will remain in continued detention.

As you may know, for those who will remain in continued detention, the Secretary announced some additional procedures that we are going to implement, and that is an Administrative Review Panel. And this will be a panel that will meet annually—it will meet more than annually. It will review each detainee's case annually to determine whether that detainee continues to pose a threat to the United States. The detainee will have the opportunity to appear in person before that panel. The detainee's foreign government will have the opportunity to submit information on the detainee's behalf. And the panel will consider all of the information, including intelligence information gained on the detainee and the information presented by the detainee and his government, and to make an independent recommendation about whether the detainee should be held.

And with that, I think we'll take any questions that you might have.

Q: Will a detainee have the right to have a lawyer when he appears before the review panel? And also, if people being held in Guantanamo pose such a threat, why not bring them to a speedy trial on charges and give them lawyers?

Butler: Well, it's important to remember that military commissions are not the reason that people are being held at Guantanamo. As I stated, under the laws of war, we have a right to hold enemy combatants who represent a threat to the United States and its forces off the battlefield. Military commissions are designed to punish those who have committed war crimes during the course of a war. And we have a process—there has been an appointing authority appointed. And I won't speak to the military commissions in too much detail, but that process will take its own course.

What we're doing is we're reviewing people to determine whether they're still a threat. And if they are determined to be a threat, then we will continue to hold them until such time that they're not a threat anymore.

Q: How about lawyers when they appear before the review panel?

Butler: The details of that haven't been worked out. There will be someone available to help the detainee understand what the process and procedures are, what the board is, but it's unclear yet what, exactly, the details of the panel will be.

Q: But as of right now, you haven't decided that this person is entitled to a lawyer when he comes before the review panel.

Butler: That's correct.

Q: Do you know when the first of these boards would meet, approximately?

Butler: Not yet. I'm not prepared to talk about that now. But it's under active review.

Q: But I mean within the next year, within the next six months?
Butler: I just can't answer that question right now. I don't know.

Q: Could you say a little bit more about the makeup of the panel, who it is going to involve, who makes the appointments? Is this something that's going to be entirely within the Department of Defense or within the administration, or will there be any kind of independent elements in this?
Butler: Again, that's all under active consideration now and I don't have any further information on the composition of the panel, who will appoint it and who will be on it.

Q: Can you say whether the panel's decision will be final, or is it subject to review in other places in the administration?
Butler: Well, the panel will make a recommendation.

Q: To whom?
Butler: That's still under consideration, but most likely to the Secretary.

Q: And so this decision is not final.
Butler: Again, the details of the panel have not yet been worked out.

Q: Could you just step back a minute and help us understand why you're here today, why the Secretary's making this speech, why, suddenly out of the clear, blue sky, so much information today about what you're doing, but yet not final information about the panel? You put it out there and you're telling us, but you're clearly undecided on any number of things. Why are you telling everybody all of this today?

Butler: Well, there's been a lot of interest in what we're doing at Guantanamo, and there have been some events in the recent past, including the transfer of the one detainee to Spain, and so we thought it was an appropriate time to share some of the information about the vigorous procedures down here that we're using at Guantanamo.

There is an elaborate process. Detainees are not in a legal black hole. There is an enormous amount of time spent scrutinizing each individual case through various agencies of the government to help us determine who these people are. We are not interested in holding anyone for one more day than we have to. We want to evaluate them. If we can reach the conclusion that they're no longer a threat, we will release them. If we believe that we can reach transfer agreements with foreign governments who will take responsibility for them so that they're no longer a threat to us or to their populations, we want to do that. So we are—we have sensed the interest in Guantanamo and we are responding to make sure that everybody is clear on what our policies are.

Q: Do you have any information that indicates anyone released from Guantanamo Bay and returned to wherever they came from has actually returned to the battlefield, so to speak, and has again joined the war on terrorism?

Butler: That's a—it's a very important concern. I'm not going to go any further than that. I don't want to get into areas that involve intelligence. Needless to say—I mentioned the Manchester Manual. When you have people that were picked up in a chaotic war, who are often trained on how to resist interrogations, who you don't have always tremendous amounts of information on before they come into your custody, you are always concerned that—you make sure that you have full information on them before they're released.

Q: Is the establishment of this panel part of a concerted effort by the U.S. military to get these detainees into the hands of foreign governments; get them out of U.S. hands and limit the numbers that are being detained at Guantanamo Bay?

Butler: No, I don't think so. The panel is designed to ensure that there is continued process that addresses the concerns that we all share that nobody be there any longer than they have to be. And if through our present procedures, the elaborate procedures that I just talked about, the detainee has not been released, these are additional procedures to make sure that—the war—the end of this war, of course—I think the secretary has alluded to this is uncertain. And one thing we can say is it's not over now, but over time we want to make sure that, even perhaps if the war ends in stages, that there's constant review of these detainees to make sure that nobody's there any longer than they have to be.

Q: Is that an acknowledgment—

Whitman: We've got time for about one or two more. And it's not often we get General Miller here, so if you have one for General Miller it might be a good time to ask him.

Q: Could I just follow with one question? Is that an acknowledgment by the Pentagon that the processes so far established—established to date, are not adequate to address those concerns of people being held too long?

Butler: Not at all. We have a certain set of processes, and as I think I mentioned to you, they're very vigorous, very elaborate. People spend enormous amounts of time scrutinizing each one of these detainees. This is just an additional procedure to once again ensure that we want to do the right thing here. We want to make sure we're holding people who are a threat and releasing people who we think no longer pose a threat.

Q: A number of these folks have been in custody two years or more now. Do they lose their intelligence value? Certainly, my two-year-old knowledge on things is dated. I mean, what kind of insight can you get on al Qaeda and their operatives?

Butler: Thank you—sir?

Miller: There are—they've had enemy combatants here at JTF Guantanamo—some for almost two years, some for as little as two months. And so as we go about determining their intelligence value and their threat, we go through this very thorough process. There are three types of intelligence: technical intelligence—that [is] what the enemy combatant was doing when he was captured, if he had a weapon; and then there is operational and strategic intelligence, that allows us to better understand how terrorists are recruited, how terrorism is sustained, how the financial networks power terrorism. And so we developed this intelligence and are continuing to develop this intelligence. We continue to get extraordinarily valuable intelligence from the detainees who are at Guantanamo.

Q: So there is an acknowledgment that if these folks have served their useful time, you're trying to figure out a way to get rid of them?

Miller: It's my responsibility to make an assessment and recommendation on the detainee's intelligence value and their risk. We do that every day and that process is ongoing. Some are getting very close for us to make a recommendation; others, who are enormously dangerous and have enormous—intelligence of enormous value, are still in this process.

Q: General, is there construction under way for a more permanent facility to house the more hard-core detainees once we seek an eventual release of the detainees?

Miller: There is another camp facility that's under construction. It is our interrogation facility which will replace the temporary facilities that we've been using for the last year and one half.

Q: How much of a number of detainees will that facility house? And—
Miller: That facility—I'm sorry. That facility—

Q: And why the construction?
Miller: That facility can house up to 100 enemy combatants who we will conduct interrogation upon. And to be frank with you, we're replacing interrogation facilities that were trailers with better facilities that allow us to more effectively and rapidly do this job of interrogation.

Q: Is it a housing facility then or is it more strictly just for interrogation?
Miller: It is a interrogation facility. But we can house an enemy combatant there to accelerate and help us in the interrogation process.

Q: Mr. Butler, why aren't some of the al Qaeda people you described being charged criminally? Because previously the U.S. government has prosecuted al Qaeda operatives, like the guy you mentioned who was at the U.S. airport shortly before 9/11?
Butler: All of these detainees were captured in the context of the global war on terrorism. They are enemy combatants in the war. There is a decision process in place, an independent appointing authority, who will eventually make decisions on who should be charged for war crimes.

But the great insight of the president, and the secretary, and others in the administration, I think, after 9/11, was that we are at war now, and that the criminal justice model, although very important to fighting the war on terrorism, is not the sole tools right now, and therefore, enemy combatants are being held for security reasons. And again, the appointing authority will decide who is charged.

Whitman: We'll take one last one, if we could. Somebody that hasn't had one.

Q: Can you tell us about what Camp Echo is, how it differs from the existing Camp Delta facility? And in connection to that, how much is the overall operation costing?
Miller: Camp Echo is our facility where we hold the pre-commission detainees.

Once the president has decided to move forward in this process, we separate these enemy combatants from the general population and move them into Camp Echo, in that facility, to allow us to separate them, plus, to allow their lawyers, when they're appointed, to have access to the enemy combatants to hold private conversations.

Q: (Off mike.) —just like Camp Delta but separate? Or is it a different layout? Well, it sounded almost like it might be a suite; there's a room for lawyers, I read somewhere. What does it look like?
Miller: There are individual buildings, so the enemy combatant is in his own cell with an area where the lawyer may come in and have a private discussion with him.

Whitman: All right, thank you very much, ladies and gentlemen.

Q: And the second part was how much is it costing?
Whitman: Who did he ask? I guess the assistant secretary?
Butler: I'm sorry, I don't have that information.
Miller: We don't normally discuss the operational costs of the JTF. It's an ongoing operational unit.

Q: Thank you.

Miller: But I will tell you we're a great buy!

White House Fact Sheet

Status of Detainees at Guantánamo
Office of the Press Secretary
February 7, 2002

United States Policy.
The United States is treating and will continue to treat all of the individuals detained at Guantánamo humanely and, to the extent appropriate and consistent with military necessity, in a manner consistent with the principles of the Third Geneva Convention of 1949.

The President has determined that the Geneva Convention applies to the Taliban detainees, but not to the al-Qaida detainees.

Al-Qaida is not a state party to the Geneva Convention; it is a foreign terrorist group. As such, its members are not entitled to POW status.

Although we never recognized the Taliban as the legitimate Afghan government, Afghanistan is a party to the Convention, and the President has determined that the Taliban are covered by the Convention. Under the terms of the Geneva Convention, however, the Taliban detainees do not qualify as POWs.

Therefore, neither the Taliban nor al-Qaida detainees are entitled to POW status.

Even though the detainees are not entitled to POW privileges, they will be provided many POW privileges as a matter of policy.

All detainees at Guantánamo are being provided:

- three meals a day that meet Muslim dietary laws
- water
- medical care
- clothing and shoes
- shelter
- showers
- soap and toilet articles
- foam sleeping pads and blankets

- towels and washcloths
- the opportunity to worship
- correspondence materials, and the means to send mail
- the ability to receive packages of food and clothing, subject to security screening

The detainees will not be subjected to physical or mental abuse or cruel treatment. The International Committee of the Red Cross has visited and will continue to be able to visit the detainees privately. The detainees will be permitted to raise concerns about their conditions and we will attempt to address those concerns consistent with security.

Housing. We are building facilities in Guantánamo more appropriate for housing the detainees on a long-term basis. The detainees now at Guantánamo are being housed in temporary open-air shelters until these more long-term facilities can be arranged. Their current shelters are reasonable in light of the serious security risk posed by these detainees and the mild climate of Cuba.

POW Privileges the Detainees will not receive. The detainees will receive much of the treatment normally afforded to POWs by the Third Geneva Convention. However, the detainees will not receive some of the specific privileges afforded to POWs, including:

- access to a canteen to purchase food, soap, and tobacco
- a monthly advance of pay
- the ability to have and consult personal financial accounts
- the ability to receive scientific equipment, musical instruments, or sports outfits

Many detainees at Guantánamo pose a severe security risk to those responsible for guarding them and to each other. Some of these individuals demonstrated how dangerous they are in uprisings at Mazar-e-Sharif and in Pakistan. The United States must take into account the need for security in establishing the conditions for detention at Guantánamo.

Background on Geneva Conventions. The Third Geneva Convention of 1949 is an international treaty designed to protect prisoners of war from inhumane treatment at the hands of their captors in conflicts covered by the Convention. It is among four treaties concluded in the wake of WWII to reduce the human suffering caused by war. These four treaties provide protections for four different classes of people: the military wounded and sick in land conflicts; the military wounded, sick and shipwrecked in conflicts at sea; military persons and civilians accompanying the armed forces in the field who are captured and qualify as prisoners of war; and civilian non-combatants who are interned or otherwise found in the hands of a party (e.g. in a military occupation) during an armed conflict.

Letter from Shafiq Rasul and Asif Iqbal to Members of the Senate Armed Services Committee

May 13, 2004

Dear Committee Member:

We were kept captive, unlawfully, by U.S. Forces in Guantánamo Bay for more than two years until the 8th March of this year. We are now back in the United Kingdom.

The legality of our detention was due to be considered by the Supreme Court when we were suddenly pulled out of Guantánamo Bay and taken to England, where we were released within 24 hours.

During the past week, we have seen with disgust the photographs of men detained and tortured in Iraq. At the same time we are reading with astonishment in the newspapers here, official statements made by the United States Government about "interrogation techniques" used at Guantánamo Bay that are completely untrue.

For instance, we read that these techniques "are meant to wear down detainees but the rules forbid the kind of tortures coming to light in Iraq." The techniques, it is said, are "designed to cause disorientation, fatigue and stress," "but there is no stripping detainees naked." There is "no physical contacts at all...our procedures prohibit us from disrobing a prisoner for any reason at all" (Army Colonel David McWilliams). It is said that "more extreme methods such as near day long interrogations require superior authorisation and medical monitoring" and that there is "no stripping or humiliation or physical abuse at Camp Delta."

Our own experience, and our close knowledge of the experience of other men detained beside us, demonstrates that each of these claims is completely untrue.

From the moment of our arrival in Guantánamo Bay (and indeed from long before) we were deliberately humiliated and degraded by the use of methods that we now read U.S. officials denying.

At Khandahar, we were questioned by U.S. soldiers on our knees, in chains, with guns held to our heads, and we were kicked and beaten. They kept us in "three-piece suits" made up of a body belt with a chain down to leg irons and hand shackles attached. Before we boarded the plane to Guantánamo, they dressed us in earmuffs, painted-out goggles and surgical masks so we were completely disoriented. On the plane, they chained us to the floor without access to a toilet for the 22-hour flight.

Our interrogations in Guantánamo, too, were conducted with us chained to the floor for hours on end in circumstances so prolonged that it was practice to have plastic chairs for the interrogators that could be easily hosed off because prisoners would be forced to urinate during the course of them and were not allowed to go to the toilet. One practice that was introduced specifically under the regime of General Miller was "short shackling" where we were forced to squat without a chair with our hands chained between our legs and chained to the floor. If we fell over, the chains would cut into our hands. We would be left in this position for hours before an interrogation, during the interrogations (which could last as long as 12 hours), and sometimes for hours while the interrogators left the room. The air conditioning was turned up so high that within minutes we would be freezing. There was strobe lighting and loud music played that was itself a form of torture. Sometimes dogs were brought in to frighten us.

We were not fed all the time that we were there, and when we were returned to our cells, we would not be fed that day.

We should point out that there were and no doubt still are cameras everywhere in the interrogation areas. We are aware that evidence that could contradict what is being said officially is in existence. We know that CCTV cameras, videotapes and photographs exist since we were regularly filmed and photographed during interrogations and at other times, as well.

They recorded the interrogations in which we were driven to make false confessions: they insisted we were the other men in a video they showed us from August 2000 with Osama bin Laden and Mohamed Atta, but we had been in England at that time. After three months in solitary confinement under harsh conditions and repeated interrogations, we finally agreed to confess. Last September an agent from MI5 came to Guantánamo with documentary evidence that proved we could not have been in Afghanistan at the time the video was made. In the end we could prove our alibis, but we worry about people from countries where records are not as available.

Soldiers told us personally of going into cells and conducting beatings with metal bars which they did not report. Soldiers told us "we can do anything we want." We ourselves witnessed a number of brutal assaults upon prisoners. One, in April 2002, was of Jummah Al-Dousari from Bahrain, a man who had become psychiatrically disturbed, who was lying on the floor of his cage immediately near to us when a group of eight or nine guards known as the ERF Team (Extreme Reaction Force) entered his cage. We saw them severely assault him. They stamped on his neck, kicked him in the stomach even though he had metal rods there as a result of an operation, and they picked up his head and smashed his face into the floor. One female officer was ordered to go into the cell and kick him and beat him which she did, in his stomach. This is known as "ERFing." Another detainee, from Yemen, was beaten up so badly that we understand he is still in hospital eighteen months later. It was suggested that he was trying to commit suicide. This was not the case.

We wish to make it clear that all of these and other incidents and all of the brutality, humiliation and degradation were clearly taking place as a result of official policies and orders.

Under the regime of General Miller, it was regular practice for detainees to have all of their hair including their beards shaved off. We were told that it was for failure to cooperate in interrogation (including if they said that you had failed a polygraph test). All of this would be filmed on video camera while it was happening. We understand that even in the face of representatives from the Red Cross having witnessed at least one such instance for themselves, the administration of the camp denied to the Red Cross that this practice existed.

Sometimes detainees would be taken to the interrogation room day after day and kept short-shackled without interrogation ever happening, sometimes for weeks on end. We received distressed reports from other detainees of their being taken to the interrogation room, left naked and chained to the floor, and of women being brought into the room who would inappropriately provoke and indeed molest them. It was completely clear to all the detainees that this was happening to particularly vulnerable prisoners, especially those who had come from the strictest of Islamic backgrounds.

Shortly before we left, a new practice was started. People would be taken to what was called the "Romeo" block where they would be stripped completely. After three days they would be given underwear. After another three days they would be given a top, and then after another three days given trouser bottoms. Some people only ever got underwear. This was said to be for "misbehaving." (Punishment within Guantánamo Bay was constantly imposed for the breaking of any camp "rule" including, for instance, having two plastic cups in your cage when you were only allowed to have one or having an extra prayer bead or too much toilet paper or excess salt). So far as leaving detainees naked is concerned, it is our understanding that the Red Cross complained to the Colonel and then the General and after that to the U.S. Administration itself about the practice.

We are completely sure that the International Red Cross has all of these complaints recorded and must undoubtedly have drawn all of them to the attention of the Administration. We therefore find it extraordinary that such lies are being told publicly today by senior officials as to the conditions and methods used at Guantánamo Bay. We are confident that records and pictures must exist and that these

should all now be provided to the public in your country as well as
ours at the earliest opportunity so that they can form their own
judgement.

  We look forward to an immediate response in view of the misinfor-
mation that is being put into the public domain worldwide and
which we know to be untrue.

Yours sincerely,
Shafiq Rasul and Asif Iqbal

We are represented by the Center for Constitutional Rights in the
United States and our solicitor, Gareth Peirce, in the United
Kingdom. Please address all inquiries to:

Michael Ratner, President
Barbara Olshansky, Deputy Legal Director
Steven Watt, Fellow
Centre for Constitutional Rights
666 Broadway
New York, NY 10012

Press Release "Officials Set Up Review Procedure for Guantánamo Detainees," American forces Press Service

By Kathleen T. Rhem
American Forces Press Service

WASHINGTON, May 19, 2004—Nearly 600 enemy combatants being held at the U.S. detention facility at Guantanamo Bay, Cuba, will now have an annual opportunity to petition for their release.

Defense officials have put into place an administrative review process to determine whether detainees should continue to be held, a senior defense official said at the Pentagon May 18.

The official explained the new procedures apply only to combatants detained in the Afghan theater and currently held at Guantanamo.

They provide for an annual review for each detainee, in which the detainee will "have an opportunity to appear before a review board and present his case for release, that he does not continue to pose a threat to the United States," the official said.

Each detainee will present his case before a panel of three military officers, and an officer will be appointed to assist in preparing his case. He also will have access to translator support as needed. Detainees' families and home countries will be invited to submit information to prove the detainee's position.

Other government agencies, including the State, Justice and Homeland Security departments and the Central Intelligence Agency, are able to submit information to the panel as well, the official explained.

The review board will make recommendations to a senior Defense Department civilian who will then decide whether to release the detainee, continue to hold him, or transfer him to his home country for continued detention there.

The briefing official said it's important to note the United States government is not legally bound to provide these reviews.

"As a matter of policy, the department has adopted these procedures so as not to keep any detainee…for whom the war is over, who is no longer a threat to the United States," he said.

Press Release "CCR Calls Guantánamo Review Policy 'Inadequate and Illegal'"

SINGLE CIVILIAN AT D.O.D. GIVEN UNBOUNDED POWER TO DETAIN FOR "ANY REASON"

MAY 19, 2004, NEW YORK—Yesterday the Department of Defense announced the release of the final Administrative Review Procedures for the continued detention of individuals at Guantánamo Bay. According to CCR's analysis, the proposed policy does nothing to bring the unlawful and arbitrary detention of foreign nationals at Guantánamo Bay into compliance with international law and the U.S. Constitution. The Center for Constitutional Rights (CCR) pointed out the serious limitations of the review procedure last month in comments to an earlier draft review procedure filed with the Department of Defense on March 29, 2004. CCR is the organization that represents the Guantánamo detainees whose case was heard by the Supreme Court on April 20th.

"The entire review procedure is inadequate and illegal," stated Rachel Meeropol, an attorney at CCR. "The only person with any power in the system is the designated civilian official or 'DCO.' He or she has the ability to order a detainee's continued detention without making any findings, meeting any criteria, or explaining his or her actions in any way. It is really just window-dressing, probably designed to give the impression to the Supreme Court, which is currently considering whether or not courts in this country have the power to review any government actions at Guantánamo, that the military is providing some process to persons it has detained without any review whatsoever for nearly two and half years."

The new policy would create a three-member review board of military officers to conduct an annual review of each individual detained at Guantánamo and make a recommendation about the continued utility of detention. The final decision as to detention is made not by the proposed review board, but by the DCO, who is appointed by the President and located in the Department of Defense. The order released yesterday actually gives the DCO even more unbounded power of detention than the draft policy, as the DCO can order continued detention based on his or her opinion that the detainee "remains a threat to the United States" or "if there is any other reason that it is in the interest of the United States and its allies" for the detainee to remain in detention. The draft procedures do not allow for any review or appeal outside the military.

Barbara Olshansky, Deputy Legal Director at CCR, also expressed concern about the narrowness of the review board's mandate. "These review boards can detain people for any reason at all. They can use coerced confessions. "Even a mere finding that someone may be a threat does not justify their detention under law. For these review panels to be at all meaningful, they must first determine each detainee's status whether according to the Geneva Convention or a parallel civil proceeding. With all that we have learned in the last few weeks about the mistreatment and torture of prisoners in U.S. custody, it is now more important then ever to fulfill our obligations under the Geneva Convention and other comparable laws."

The final order does respond to some of CCR's criticism of the policies regarding notice to the detainee and presentation of evidence to the three-member review board. However, since the DCO continues to be the only individual with any power in the system, these changes will not have any real impact on the outcome of the review procedure.

APPENDIX TWO

FURTHER READING

Jimmy Carter, "The Seeds of A Rights Scandal in Iraq," *The Washington Post,* May 14, 2004.

Nancy Chang, Center for Constitutional Rights, *Silencing Political Dissent: How Post-September 11 Anti-Terrorism Measures Threaten Our Civil Liberties.* New York: Seven Stories Press/ Open Media Series, 2002.

David Cole, Center for Constitutional Rights Board Member, *Enemy Aliens.* New York: The New Press, 2003.

David Cole, Center for Constitutional Rights Board Member, "Guantánamo Continues as a Blot of Shame on the U.S.," *The Los Angeles Times,* February 22, 2004.

David Cole, Center for Constitutional Rights Board Member, and James X. Dempsey, *Terrorism and the Constitution.* New York: The New Press, 2002.

Greg Miller, "Many Held at Guantánamo Not Likely Terrorists," *The Los Angeles Times,* December 22, 2002.

George Monbiot, "One Rule For Them," *The Guardian,* March 25, 2003.

Barbara Olshansky, Center for Constitutional Rights, *Secret Trials and Execution: Military Tribunals and the Threat to Democracy.* New York: Seven Stories Press/ Open Media Series, 2002.

Michael Ratner, Center for Constitutional Rights President, *Making Us Less Free: War on Terrorism or War on Liberty?* At www.humanrightsnow.org.

Michael Ratner, Center for Constitutional Rights President, *War Crime Not Self-Defense: the Unlawful War Against Iraq.* At www.humanrightsnow.org.

David Rose, "Inside Guantánamo: How We Survived Jail Hell," *The Observer,* March 14, 2004.

WEB SITES WITH MORE INFORMATION

Center for Constitutional Rights
www.ccr-ny.org
Updates on Guantánamo Bay cases and other CCR detention cases, with a focus on international human rights and civil liberties. CCR provides legal assistance to U.S. detainees.

Institute for Media Analysis
www.covertaction.org
The Institute for Media Analysis, Inc., was established in 1986 with the primary purpose of providing to the public educational materials relating to the workings of government and of the media, and in particular the relations between the two.

Amnesty International
www.ai.org
Examines the human rights violations that are inherent in the Guantánamo Bay detentions.

Cageprisoners.com
www.cageprisoners.com
This website exists solely to raise awareness of the plight of the cage

prisoners at Guantánamo Bay, through effective legal means. The website is not aligned to any Islamic group or organization. The site is run by individual Muslim volunteers and supported by both Muslim and non-Muslim lawyers, scholars, doctors, and academics.

Human Rights Watch
www.hrw.org
Monitors and provides reports of human rights violations from around the globe.

Rasul V. Bush
www.ccr-ny.org/rasul/
Reports on the Supreme Court case challenging the detentions at Guantánamo.

Guantánamo Human Rights Organization
www.guantanamohrc.org
The London-based Commission's long-term objective is to achieve an end to all forms of internment without trial, whether in Guantánamo, or in Britain in Belmarsh and Woodhill, or on the island of Diego Garcia.

The Guantánamobile Project
www.guantánamobile.org
An attempt to inform and collect public opinion about U.S. detention of prisoners at Guantánamo Bay, Cuba. The administration's decision to detain prisoners has grave implications for human rights and civil liberties.

United Nations
www.un.org
Voluminous material on international law and treaties.

About the Authors

Michael Ratner is President of the Center for Constitutional Rights. He serves as co-counsel in *Rasul v. Bush*, the historic case of Guantánamo detainees before the U.S. Supreme Court.

Under Ratner's leadership, the Center has aggressively challenged the constitutional and international law violations undertaken by the United States post-9/11, including the constitutionality of indefinite detention and the restrictions on civil liberties as defined by the unfolding terms of a permanent war. In the 1990s Ratner acted as a principal counsel in the successful suit to close the camp for HIV-positive Haitian refugees on Guantánamo Bay. He has written and consulted extensively on Guantánamo, the Patriot Act, military tribunals, and civil liberties in the post-9/11 world.

He has also been a lecturer of international human rights litigation at the Yale Law School and the Columbia School of Law, president of the National Lawyers Guild, special Counsel to Haitian President Jean-Bertrand Aristide to assist in the prosecution of human rights crimes, and radio co-host for the civil rights show *Law and Disorder*.

Ellen Ray is President of the Institute for Media Analysis and the author and editor of numerous books and magazines on U.S. intelligence and international politics. She is co-editor with William Schaap of *Bioterror: Manufacturing Wars the American Way* and *Covert Action: The Root of Terrorism*, both published by Ocean Press in 2003.

Chelsea Green is committed to being a sustainable business enterprise as well as a publisher of books on the politics and practice of sustainability. This means reducing natural resource and energy use to the maximum extent possible. We print our books and catalogs on chlorine-free recycled paper, using soy-based inks, whenever possible. *Guantánamo: What the World Should Know* was printed on Legacy Trade Book Natural, a 100 percent post-consumer waste recycled, old growth forest-free paper supplied by Webcom.

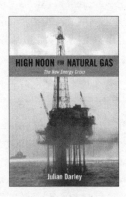